RAISING A FORERUNNER
G E N E R A T I O N

RAISING A FORERUNNER
GENERATION

CHILDREN WITH A PASSION FOR JESUS

LELONNIE HIBBERD

First published in 2003 by

KEVIN MAYHEW LTD
Buxhall, Stowmarket, Suffolk, IP14 3BW
E-mail: info@kevinmayhewltd.com

KINGSGATE PUBLISHING INC
1000 Pannell Street, Suite G, Columbia, MO 65201
E-mail: sales@kingsgatepublishing.com

9 8 7 6 5 4 3 2 1 0

ISBN 1 84417 103 5
Catalogue No 1500604

Cover design by Angela Selfe
Typeset by Fiona Connell-Finch

Printed and bound in Great Britain

This book is for you, Lord
With all my love

My deepest thanks:

To Mike – my precious husband – full of grace, generosity, fun, creativity, spontaneity and great encouragement.

To Danny, Jacquie and Charlie

Each of you is unique and a delight – you all light up my life with love and laughter.
You are the best!

Acknowledgements

The publishers are grateful to the following for permission to reproduce the copyrights they control:

CopyCare Ltd for the chorus to *I want to know you* by Brian Doerksen and Cindy Rethmeier, copyright © 1990 Mercy/Vineyard Publishing, administered by CopyCare, PO Box 77, Hailsham, BN27 3EF. music@copycare.com. Used by permission.

Noel Richards and Sovereign Lifestyle Music Ltd for the words to *Heroes* by Gerald Coates and Noel Richards, copyright © 1986 Sovereign Lifestyle Music Ltd, PO Box 356, Leighton Buzzard, LU7 3WP, UK. Reproduced by permission.

Tyndale House for the quote from *Faith Training* by Joe White, copyright © 1996 Joe White, and published by Tyndale House.

Every effort has been made to trace the owners of copyright material and it is hoped that no copyright has been infringed. Pardon is sought and apology made if the contrary be the case and a correction will be made in any reprint of this book.

Contents

Prologue

I saw a vision of Jesus. He was like a rainbow, his clothes were like a rainbow, and he was like the sunrise. He was the sunrise! His clothes in pattern and texture and colour were more amazing than anything I had ever seen; they were full of light. Light was shining on them too, as though spotlights were on him. It was darkness around him but he was lighting it up.

It was windy and his hair was being blown in the wind and his garments were being blown in the wind. But the wind was fire and the fire was wind.

He was standing on a high place and his arms were outstretched not in command but in invitation. The invitation was full of glory and light. He was so beautiful, so compelling, his love was awesome and all things were drawn to him. As they responded; as every created thing and every person responded to his majesty and his beauty, they seemed to be caught up in the whirlwind of his glory and his love and rushed towards him, in response. He was their heart's desire.

Foreword – A Guide for Parents

Ages of Children and Young People Covered by this Book

This book covers children from birth and into the teenage years. Foundations will be established through faith training from the youngest age, which can be built on right into young adulthood. We can pray over our children when they are newborn, we can worship with baby in our arms. We can tell them the stories of Jesus from as young as six months old. The name Jesus can be among the first our children learn. Praying children grow into praying older children, who in turn grow into praying teens, providing we continually stimulate and encourage opportunities for creative prayer.

There is no Condemnation

Read through the book and let the Holy Spirit speak to your heart. There may be times when you may feel a sense of regret or defensiveness because of what you have not imparted to your children. These are the times to lay burdens and regrets at the cross, and remember that no situation is irredeemable. As you read, there will hopefully be more times when you will feel a release from heavy burdens, which may have dogged you for years. Yield to God throughout the reading of this book and allow the Holy Spirit to touch, to inspire and to heal you. Receive the grace of God into your life; that grace which can cover all our mistakes, if we allow it to. Receive God's grace as you read. A voice in your mind may shout that you have failed with your children, but your reply can be, 'Praise God, I have failed, but his strength is made perfect in my weakness.' The greater your failure, the more you qualify for the grace of God. It is never too late to impart kingdom truths to your children, whatever age they are.

Pray Without Ceasing

The reader may wonder, 'How can I do all that is mentioned in this book? That would consume my whole life and we wouldn't have time for anything else.' This book is not meant to encourage the reader to 'do and do and do even more'; it is not a book about doing the right thing. We are not advocating doing one or two or ten 'God slots' with your children each day.

This is meant to be a book to encourage the reader to know the Lord ('I want to know Christ...' Philippians 3:10). Knowing the Lord allows us to be filled more and more with him, and so then we will naturally reflect more and more of his heart in every circumstance and situation. It will come naturally as breathing. Make no mistake – we *will* impart to our children who we are, whether we are filled with a holy or an unholy Spirit. This book is meant simply to stimulate and to encourage the reader to tap into the awesome and infinite creativity of God the Holy Spirit.

The Bible admonishes us to 'Pray without ceasing' precisely because it *is* possible to do so as we go on being filled with the Holy Spirit. So it is the author's belief that we can 'Impart the kingdom to our children – without ceasing'.

The author of the book of Deuteronomy put it so well (Deuteronomy 6:7-9) when he said, 'These commandments that I give you today are to be upon your hearts. Impress them on your children. Talk about them when you sit at home and when you walk along the road, when you lie down and when you get up. Tie them as symbols on your hands and bind them on your foreheads. Write them on the door-frames of your houses and on your gates.' The author of Deuteronomy does not seem to leave out any waking or sleeping moment. We are to be full of the presence of the Lord so that in every aspect of our lives we can naturally share his presence and his heart with our children. The added blessing we live under is that in our times, we have the Holy Spirit to help us – we don't have to do it on our own!

Freedom and Creativity

Do not use this book religiously. Do not work through it from start to finish, implementing it in your home point by point. Start somewhere, where you feel it is relevant to your present circumstances. Practise sharing Jesus with your children a little at a time and don't try to 'do it all' at once. Many of the ideas in this book may spark your own ideas. You may think, 'Actually, what I'd rather do is . . .' or 'Why not extend that idea to a different situation, which is more relevant for us?' or 'Why don't we try this instead?'

Most importantly, grow in your own intimacy with the Lord Jesus and rely on the Holy Spirit's inspiration every step of the way. It's easy to share stories about Jesus with your children, even if you don't know him very well, but you will not be able to share God's heart or bring life to those stories because they will not be relevant to your own life or that of your family.

Repetition

There is a good deal of repetition in the book, because there are certain truths about wonderful facets of Jesus' character, or God the Father's character or even the Holy Spirit, which we can learn over and over again. These immutable truths will apply to many situations and may help us in different ways and in different contexts. For example, learning to use, to apply and to love the word of God is mentioned time and time again throughout the chapters. Each time, the author has been impressed by the wonder of God's word in a slightly different way as it has applied in a different situation. Each time there has been a new sense of revelation or insight into the beauty and immense treasure contained within the word of God.

Fan into Flame the Gift that is within you

The book is meant to provoke and to inspire parents – to prayer, to humility, to honesty, to worship. Every parent has a creative gift from God and as we begin to seek him for ourselves and for our children, we will be amazed at his response, amazed at the creativity that comes out of us and amazed at the creativity we see in our children.

Personal Experience

To encourage the reader, all the ideas shared in this book have come from personal experience, either of the author or of friends or other people known to the author. The ideas shared in this book are really possible; they really work. The book is based on real situations, real occurrences and real outcomes. When coupled with the reader's responses to the Lord Jesus in every situation, these ideas have the potential to effect profound and wonderful results.

This book comes with the author's heartfelt prayer for every reader: that there will be a mighty rising up of a whole generation, a mighty taking back of long lost ground, and a mighty standing together across the generations – for the gospel and to herald the Coming King.

LELONNIE HIBBERD

Introduction

I See Children of Destiny

One day one generation will take the gospel to the ends of the earth. You and I have one life to live, one chance to be that generation, or one chance to influence that generation. Each individual is born for a unique purpose and with a God-given destiny. I see the anointing on them; I see their potential; I see their destiny. In some of the children I see specific things, in others there is just an overwhelming sense of destiny. God help us to see what is in our children, what he sees in them, then to encourage them, and to pray for them and to stand with them. I see in this generation of children and young people, history makers, people who have within them the potential to change the course of history, to affect every nation on this earth. Could this be that Kairos time when the Lord's purposes are accomplished across the earth not only by each generation fulfilling its God-given purpose, but also by all the generations standing together, as in Malachi 4:6.

I See a Battle and a Baton

There is an enemy who not only knows the potential of the young people of this generation but also who has a clear, defined strategy to systematically destroy individuals in body, mind and spirit. We need only look at how many children die needlessly as a result of war, AIDS, famine, abortion, poverty and all forms of abuse. Our children were born into a battle: a battle for their very existence and calling. Let's make no mistake, our children are on this enemy's hit list. It is not a question of whether or not we choose to enter that battle. It is raging around your children and mine as we live and as you read these words. There are agendas, battle plans and objectives against our children and young people. The question is: will we or will we not give them the strategy, the weapons and the armour they need to stand and advance in this battle? To do nothing is to set them up for defeat.

I also see the children's great need of our sincere prayers and our standing in agreement with God's word, our encouragement and our faith, our wisdom and our experience. For us to do nothing could be devastating. God help us to pray consistently, confidently and fervently, for our own children and for the children of the nations, to use all the spiritual resources at our disposal to cover the emerging generations with powerful and effective prayer. Why not, for example, target and cover in prayer the potential victims of abduction or child pornography before those crimes happen? Surely our God is able to protect those children. This is surely part of our destiny, to connect by prayer with the power and resources of heaven to help all children to enter into their destiny.

I see a baton like a baton in a relay race. The baton is the faith; it's knowing Jesus and all he is. Since our children were babies they have lived on our faith; we continue to share our faith and hold the baton for them, but one day they must each take it up for themselves. This in itself is in the midst of battle. I feel that in spite of all our sincerity and passion for our children we sometimes pass on the wrong baton. It's often unspoken but our children pick up a message that they must live under countless expectations to live like a Christian. Each expectation places such a heavy weight on them. And, of course, they must fail, because they, like us, are not perfect. They must buckle under the weight. By placing heavy expectations on our children, by giving them many rules by which they must live, we are setting them up to fail, as they must fail, for we all make mistakes, each day of our lives.

Imagine yourself carrying a backpack. Imagine each of the following rules is like a different heavy load you are required to carry in that backpack. Don't lie (a heavy load), don't ever swear, don't succumb to temptations of drugs, bullying, pride, don't follow the crowd for goodness' sake, be a leader, pray regularly, more than once a day if possible, read your Bible, better yet, learn lots of Bible verses, share Jesus without embarrassment . . . and so on. How can our children succeed at successfully following all these rules if they don't even know how to live by faith in Jesus? How can they succeed if they are doing it all in their own strength? Jesus said, 'My yoke is easy' (Matthew 11:29), yet we burden our children with such a weight of expectations about how they should live, without them ever being taught how it is possible. We require them to 'live a godly' or, even worse, 'a good life' without building into their lives the foundations to carry them through the storms and injustices, the anxieties and disappointments they will surely face.

I believe there is a real baton to pass on to our children, but it can be none other than Jesus himself. We can pass on to our children a set of beliefs and a set of rules to live by, which they may or may not succeed at in varying degrees, depending on the temptations they encounter. We can share our love for Jesus and our understanding of him, which they can listen to but not always identify with. *We cannot give them a personal and powerful encounter with Jesus.* Unless they meet Jesus for themselves, they may find it increasingly difficult to live the Christian life. When our children fail (and they will fail, for that is the nature of the human heart), unless they know the Lord Jesus enough to know his love for them even in the midst of their weakness and failure, disillusionment can quickly set in. Our children need to know that living a Christian life is not by might (by their strength of character) or by power (their strength of will to resist temptation) but by the power of the Holy Spirit. The Bible is full of verses which show that the business of living as a Christian is by the power of God and not by our goodness (God is at work in us to will and to act according to his good pleasure: Philippians 2:13); (His strength is made perfect in our weakness: 2 Corinthians 12:9); (He who began a good work in you will carry it on to completion: Philippians 1:6).

Even Paul says in Romans: 'For I have the desire to do what is good, but I cannot carry it out' (Romans 7:18b) and then he says, 'What a wretched person I am! Who will rescue me.' (Romans 7:24) and finally goes on in chapters 7 and 8 to explain that we *can* live a holy life, *through* the Spirit of God who lives in us.

So let's go back to the backpack: imagine your child, nearly bent over double with the heavy weight on their shoulders; imagine saying to them, as you take the heavy weights off, one by one: 'All I ask of you is one thing, desire to know Jesus.' Put in other ways, but the same one thing: 'Desire to see him, look for him, ask him to come into your life, ask to see him, ask to hear from him, ask for his touch, ask God to help you to love Jesus.' Soon there will be no weight of expectations – the backpack will feel very light and your children will feel free. Tell them, 'You are not able to live a holy life, but Jesus is completely able to help you to succeed. He is able to give you all the faith you will need, all the power and all the strength. You may fail along the way, but Jesus said, "My grace is sufficient", that means it's *enough* to cover your every failure.'

Our children need to see Jesus with their own eyes, to hear his voice into their own hearts, to feel his touch with their own senses, to be in his presence themselves. When this happens, watch the temptations fall off them like dust blown away in the wind!

Therefore, the most important thing we can do is to pray, believing that Jesus comes to our children and young people. The most important thing we can teach and pass on and model is not a set of rules, but Jesus himself: a passion for Jesus, a desire for an encounter with Jesus, a relationship with Jesus, a vision of Jesus. This is a dangerous and costly prayer because the Lord may require you to be part of his response to your children. The challenge for you and me as parents is therefore: 'Do I have passion for Jesus? Do I know him? Do I know his love or his touch in my life? Can my children see Jesus in me, in my day-to-day life, in my relationship with my spouse and with them?'

I See an Army and a Great Cost

I have literally seen in a vision an army of children and young people advancing across the face of this earth. You couldn't count them. They were relentless. Their weapons were prayer, faith, miracles, and they devoured all evil in their path. Our children are called to be part of that army.

As I saw the vision the words burned in my mind: 'who

did not love their lives'. I looked it up and found a scripture in Revelation 12:11, which reads, 'They overcame him [the enemy, Satan, the accuser] by the blood of the Lamb and by the word of their testimony; they did not love their lives so much as to shrink from death.'

I see a great cost. On more than one occasion when I have been praying for the children and young people of the nations, that they would rise up and be filled with power and anointing, Jesus has said to me: 'Can you pay the cost? Do you know the cost?' Finally, I have seen the cost, I have seen pain, I have seen suffering and I wonder, can I pay the cost? Then I turn to Jesus – who for the joy set before him endured the cross. As I look at him I see that there is a joy set before us too, there is a joy set before our children, which is so awesome that they will literally love not their lives. I see martyrs, but I have also seen the glory of Jesus. The cost is great but the presence of God is far, far greater and far more glorious. I believe these are days when the emerging generations will literally see the heavens opened and will see the glory of Jesus. The cost will be as nothing in comparison.

There is a kind of analogy in the history of North America. They have glorious stories of the pioneers: such adventure, such excitement, such courage and bravery, such colourful tales of life lived to the full are told of people who hacked a future for a nation out of the wilderness. But that's how we see it today. If you go deeper and learn how the pioneers really lived, you will see a different story. The pioneers were the ones who were orphaned, tortured, widowed, broken, lost, maimed and burned alive. They paid for the freedom of the future with their lives; they sacrificed comfort and security for a greater hope. Their story – glorious though it was – didn't feel glorious as they were living it.

So it is with people of destiny; we have no promises of physical prosperity, no guarantees that we will even reach our destination. We may even travel a lonely and difficult road because the nature of pioneering and the nature of following Jesus is that no one has gone your journey before you. But we have the firm and unchanging promise of the presence of Jesus with us. I have come to the conclusion that the presence of Jesus must make any hardship pale in comparison.

So though there may be a great cost in terms of comfort, security, suffering, there is a far greater joy, hope and presence of Jesus. There is a far greater vision to see the redeemed coming out of every tribe and nation, which I believe will literally capture the hearts of children and young people in a way that we have only dreamed of.

I See Jesus

The centre of it all, the reason for it all, the goal of it all: we must see Jesus, we must see more than we have seen, and we must hunger for his presence. I see a generation who will be so radical in going after the presence of Jesus that their daily heart cry will echo the words of an old Vineyard song by Brian Doerksen and Cindy Rethmeier (© 1990, Mercy/Vineyard Publishing/Copycare):

> I want to know you, I want to love you, I want to be found in you, I want to be clothed in your truth, so I'll fix my eyes on you, Lord I must see you, I'll put my faith in you, I'll spend my life on you, I want to know you, I want to love you . . . Jesus

This is something we cannot muster up in ourselves and this is something we must not feel guilty about not feeling. In his great grace and mercy, I believe that God himself is committed to pouring out passion for his Son in the hearts and lives of his people because it was one of Jesus' last, heartfelt prayers when he was alone with his Father and before he went to the cross (John 17:26).

Whatever the future holds for our children, whatever calling the Lord puts on their lives, whatever destiny he gives each to fulfil, I believe that in practice, in the earth, in the lives of this generation, the pursuit of the presence of Jesus will be by far the largest, most passionate, most radical, most single-minded pursuit of all.

I See Parents in Partnership

God has given these young people to you and me to raise, to mentor, to love, to release. I see your calling, your significance, your uniqueness, your importance, your own potential. I see you first of all knowing Jesus like you have never done before, then teaching, modelling and living by faith yourselves. I see you warring over your children, fighting in prayer that they take the ground, subdue nations and advance the kingdom. I see parents with the same spirit on them as Mary the mother of Jesus had. Parents who experience all at once the tears and the laughter, the sadness and the joy, the glory and the pain, 'the sword piercing her heart', as they release their children to the purposes of God. There is a tremendous opportunity and the potential for a tremendous partnership for us to stand with our children and to serve them in the battle: by prayer and by our lives to help to equip them each day.

It starts in the home, when everybody is grumpy, when there's disagreement, anger, jealousy, when it's not glorious, when it's mundane and boring. There is a challenge to parents – to make our lives, not when we're at meetings, but our lives at home, in the bedroom, with spouses, with people in the church whom we find totally exasperating, at our job, when out with friends, at school – to make our lives an act of worship. We sing on a Sunday about offering up our lives to the Lord and pouring out our love and worship to him; we sing about total surrender. ('I will offer up my life' by Matt Redman, © Unveiled Music/Kingsway, 1994). These words are only outworked and lived in day-to-day life. It is then that these words become either our opportunity to demonstrate a living faith, or an obstacle we trip over.

Parents in partnership can also mean parents encouraging parents, rather than one-upmanship or parents competing with parents. Insecurity can cause us to feel good when others fail and what can bring out more insecurity than being a parent? I believe God has given us everything and is requiring everything in return. We are literally called to be right with God, to yield to God continually.

So as parents, I believe we need to give encouragement and honour to each other. We need to give other parents the space to be different to us. We need to break the Pharisee thing, which says, *Thank God my kids aren't quite as bad as theirs, at least my kids are OK in that area.* God has challenged me to esteem others' children as my own and to pray for them with a sense of responsibility as though they were in my family. If there is a problem with your children, it's my problem, too, in the sense that the very least I can do is to pray with humility. Humility means knowing that every success I have with my own children is solely because of the grace and kindness of God and not my own merit.

We need to stand together as parents to tackle our problems. It is so good to keep being open to advice or another perspective from those we are in close relationship with. True security, which comes from Jesus, allows us to be able to learn from others and to recognise that 'I don't always have all the answers.'

I See Family

There has been lots of talk in recent years about children needing mentors, that is, people other than biological parents who have spiritual or relational input into those children's lives. I believe God has mentors for our children and young people – and there are people he wants to include in your and my family. There are people in your church family who need to be listened to because they have treasure to impart out of their experience with their own children, or because of what God has put on their hearts. This is all very good and is not a new concept.

But when speaking about family, I am speaking about something else. In order to understand we may need to break our mindsets. We can sometimes only receive what God is saying through our spirits and not through the words coming into our minds. We need to yield our strong reactions to God and not rely on our own understanding, but be in humility.

I see that God is bringing a new order of family on the earth in the coming years. The word family is so emotive and brings so many things to mind. But to see what God is saying, we have to literally get out of our boxes and lay down our ingrained definitions.

I am not trying to take away anything good and wonderful that biological parents have. I am not trying to rob you and me of status and I am not trying to belittle the experience of many years, which can be such a blessing to many people. This is not about status, or experience. This is not to take what is good from biological parents, but to add to the good to make it better.

This is a gift from God to the earth. There are too many orphans for just the biological parents. There are too many lost, broken and abused children for just the married people.

I believe God himself is going to redefine the words father, mother, son and daughter. He is going to widen – not water down – but widen the inclusivity of the words. God is going to add a practical anointing of father and mother to his church, which is going to include single people, and married people who have never given birth to biological children. The anointing of parenting, which comes from God, will not just be mentoring, though mentoring will of course be part of it. The anointing of being a father or mother which comes from God will be in its effect as significant as biological parenting, and in some cases more so.

There will be much that these 'new' parents can learn from the experience and perspectives of biological parents. But equally there will be much that biological parents will learn from these 'new' parents.

If God can make a child to be born from a virgin, then surely he can make a young person who has never physically fathered or given birth to a child a father or mother after his own heart.

I See Prayer

I see new ways of prayer. I see prayer being enlarged and breaking out until it is unrecognisable when compared with our current definitions of prayer. I remember praying with a friend many years ago, 'God help us to *be* prayer, to *live* prayer.'

The way we pray is not wrong; it is good, it is wonderful but it is not enough for the coming days. God wants a people of powerful and persistent prayer who will not back off.

I see new people having an anointing of prayer. We need to humbly learn from them. Learning from the artist, for example, who practises prayer while he creates his art. But I also see God birthing creativity in everyone in the area of prayer. We need to learn to pray without ceasing.

We need to learn to carry our children in prayer in countless and creative ways – we need to rely upon, ask for and learn to receive the very inspiration of heaven.

We need to learn the relationship between intercession and worship. We need to learn to live in the presence of God. We need a prayer life that can stand astride the practical and the spiritual all at once.

I see prayer as a key to ourselves and our children finding our destiny in God.

And with respect to prayer and all that is written here, I see Jesus' total and utter faithfulness and ability to take us into these uncharted waters, into these new places. He only asks that we love him and yield ourselves to him.

Hearing from God

Children can hear from God, no matter what their age. At the outset, the most important encouragement the author can give parents is to please learn to treasure God's word. The Bible says that God 'has exalted above all things, his Name and his word' (Psalm 138:2). This Scripture must give us an idea of how important his own word is to God himself. How important should it then be to us? I am speaking about the written word of God found in Scripture and about living words from God you have received in your own heart or through trusted others. Delight in the word of God, love it, receive it, honour it, refer to it. Following are ways in which parents and guardians can help children to develop this ability naturally.

- Give your children regular opportunities, as part of your prayer time, for example, where they can practise hearing from God. Practise first at home and later when you are praying with friends.

- Grown-ups often have a problem with God speaking to children because they can hardly believe it can happen. But children don't have a problem with it and neither does God! He loves speaking to little children; he loves giving them prophetic words or words of knowledge, which astound us adults. He loves answering their prayers of faith and healing the sick through them.

• Why not begin by praying for your children, that God will speak to them and help them to know him and to walk with him? Ask God to give you eyes to see and discernment to know when he is speaking to your children.

• Find Scriptures that show God speaking to children (Samuel, Jeremiah, etc.) and read them with your children. Find other Scriptures that describe God speaking to people of all ages (Exodus 3:1-10; 1 Samuel 3; Jeremiah 1:4-9; Genesis 40 and 41; Daniel 4:19-27; Acts 9: 4-6 and Acts 10: 9-16, to mention a few examples). It was a very normal part of life to some Old Testament characters and there is no reason why it shouldn't be a normal part of life for us too. After all, God is for us, and he loves to speak with us. Sometimes he did not even act without first talking about his plans with his servants or the prophets (Hebrews 1:1; Genesis 18). Scriptures such as those mentioned above will help your children to become both familiar with what it's like to hear from God and expectant that they too can hear from him.

• You can explain to children *how* God speaks to us when we hear his word from the Bible; for example, that sometimes we read a certain passage or verse and it seems to jump out at us, as though it was 'written just for me'. Sometimes the verse or passage seems so amazingly relevant to our current personal situation or it seems to answer a cry or prayer of our heart. If you recognise that a Scripture or passage you are reading with your children is God speaking into a family question or situation or problem, tell them so and explain:

'God is speaking to us through this passage and this is what I think he is saying.' The next time it happens you might say to your child, 'I think God is speaking to us through these verses; what do you think he is saying to us?'

Example:

A young teenage boy we know was being bullied in school and the parents were learning to deal with it, situation by situation. On one particular day, the 13-year-old came home particularly upset at what had occurred in school. As his parents and his older sister began to pray with him, his older sister rushed upstairs and came down with her Bible. She proceeded to read the most amazing encouragement to her brother from a Bible passage that seemed to fit his situation to a T. His parents then encouraged him, 'Look at what the Lord has prepared for you today – he knew what you'd be going through and he gave these words to your sister to give to you.' Then the parents gave their son some instruction. 'You need to meditate on these words. Read them each day for a few days. Think about them and actively receive the promises. Let the words sink into your spirit and bring healing to your heart.' Needless to say the boy's sister was also incredibly encouraged.

- You can encourage your children to hear God's voice in their mind or heart, simply by practice. The younger the child the easier this will be. We have had experiences where we have told very young children (say 5-7 years) that God loves to speak to children. We have asked them to close their eyes, listen to God for a minute or two and that he is going to speak to them. The children simply believe it, respond to God with faith, and he gives them some amazing words and pictures. You can do the same at home.

- You will need to explain to your children the different ways God could speak, and try to explain what it may be like. We explained something like this: 'You may see a picture in your mind, just tell us what the picture is about. You may see a picture in your mind and you may then ask God what it means. You may hear words in your mind as though someone was telling you something. You may feel a feeling along with certain words or thoughts in your mind.' It's important to be with our children as they begin to practise hearing from God. They always wonder, 'How do I know it's God?' We can help them learn to recognise God's voice through our own experience of hearing from God and through our encouragement when we know God has spoken to them. In our own family, we as parents rarely fail to share it with our children, when the Lord speaks to us. It's usually very exciting, how can we keep it from our children and deny them the opportunity to bless God for his goodness?

Example:

A boy we know heard the audible voice of God at age 4, after praying with his mother for nine months beforehand, 'Lord can I please hear your voice, like a real voice.' The Lord spoke audibly to the child nine times in one day and the parents faithfully recorded every word. That experience is a great source of encouragement to the whole family today. They can look back on what God said to their son; and he can read the wonderful words of love and acceptance God gave to him.

- It's important to encourage your child and if he or she doesn't hear from the Lord to begin with, to say, 'That's all right, let's try again tomorrow.' Don't make it a pressure or a worry; it should be a wonderful and a natural experience. The younger your child, the easier he or she will be able to hear from God. Our children began to hear the Lord's voice from age 2-3.

- Encourage your child to *desire* to hear from God. Why? First, because it is a wonderful experience: God speaks to express his love for us, to teach us, to help us in our life, to guide us, to help us to help each other and to help us to know him better.

  Second, because God *desires* to speak to us for all of the above reasons. The Bible is bursting with stories of God's relationship with humankind. God spoke with ordinary people of all ages to express aspects of himself. He expressed his heart to Paul and Timothy, his will to Moses, his plans to Samuel and to Abraham, and his love to King David and the apostle John. These are just a few of many examples.

  The third reason to teach our children to desire to hear from God is because we were created for fellowship with our Creator and true relationship, true fellowship or true friendship is two-way. Both parties express themselves and listen to the other.

- We are often proficient at speaking to God, at asking, even at complaining and expressing dissatisfaction with our situation. We call this being real with God and there is nothing wrong with it. On the contrary, it is commendable and even necessary to be able to be completely honest with God. But how often do we just stop to listen to our Father, our Friend, our Lover, our Saviour, our Master, our Lord? How often do we listen to his expressions of his heart, his desires, his pain, his vision, *his* will? Therefore, the listening element of our relationship with God is as important to pass on to our children, as is our need to be honest with him.

Gifts

Helping our children live both recognising and using the gifts God has given them.

Following are a few very simple but foundational background observations on the whole area of gifts and giving. Following that are suggestions inspired by and based upon the Parable of the Ten Talents (Luke 19).

Background Observations

- The more we use what God has given us, the more he gives us.

- Whatever gift God has given you, give it away. God will give you back even more.

  Example:

  A family we know felt God was asking them to give away some money they had just received. They had been looking forward to that money and to what they would buy with it. They gave it away and within three months had unexpectedly received back three times what they had given.

- We need to simply use whatever gifts we have and do our best. It is unhelpful to compare our gifts with those of others or to judge the outward performance of others because of our perception of the worth of their gifts. In other words, it is unhelpful to think, God *has given that person such a great preaching gift. I could never be like her, my gift is not nearly so good, or exciting or 'public' as hers* . . . Our children will pick up on this kind of attitude even if it is largely unspoken. If we aim for Christian maturity, then the time has come to no longer entertain such thoughts. If we believe that God made each of us wonderfully and uniquely, as in Psalm 139, then why not rather find out about the gifts he has given *us*, and use them to the best of our ability?

- It's so important to use our gifts, even if we get tired of doing so, or discouraged, or if we don't see much fruit. We need to persevere and use what God has given us; so often we judge our gift to be less exciting or smaller or less important than someone else's gift. This kind of attitude will not only hamper our effective use of our own gift, but will also grow in us a mistrust of God's plan and creative purpose for us. We can also measure ourselves against everyone else, forgetting that God made us to serve him in a unique way, which may not be like anyone else around us.

Example:

A lady I know used to compare herself with the neighbour around the corner. The neighbour always seemed to be pouring herself out on behalf of the poor and needy, she seemed to be such an amazing woman and she was. The lady spent a number of years feeling guilty because she knew she could never counsel people or spend time with them like her neighbour did. One day she finally heard the Lord's voice and realised that he had never asked her to be a carbon copy of her neighbour.

She was good with children and used to entertain her own and friends' children on many occasions. Finally she began to realise that the thing she was both good at and loved doing was the very thing the Lord was asking of her. This seems so simple an example, but even as adults so many of us are caught up comparing ourselves with others and feeling guilty because we don't measure up. God help us to see the unique gifts he has bestowed upon each of us. God help us to use our talents with joy and freedom, being thankful that we are able to serve him. God forgive us for comparing ourselves with others, and living in self-condemnation and unfruitfulness. In order to impart this freedom to our children we must be able to live in it ourselves.

- God is a God of love even though he requires much of those to whom much is given. His heart is to give, to bless and to reward – in proportion to his grace and mercy and not in proportion to our good deeds.

- Fear of failure is no way to live a life; it binds us up and twists our attitudes and renders us useless so that we won't even try. There is no problem with failure if we do our best; in fact it is only when we step out in faith and use the gifts God has given us, that he can use us, increase our gifts and bless others through us. God has been very clear with the author and her own family. In our own lives, he has never convicted us for failing, which we have done – so often. On the contrary, we have been amazed at the times when we have failed, knowing we did our best. It was during these times that the Lord's grace and love and favour was showered upon us *as though we had succeeded.*

- It is far better to have stepped out in faith and failed than to have sat back and done nothing. We know people who have stepped out in faith even to the point of taking risks to follow the Lord in what they honestly felt he was asking of them. All this was done after speaking with, praying with and receiving advice from close friends who were prepared to walk the whole journey with them and to support them whatever the outcome. When they sometimes failed, all they heard the Lord saying to them was, 'I never required you to succeed in the way you felt you should, I only required your obedience and that you did your best.'

- We don't have to *feel* confident to be used by God; we just have to be *willing* to serve him and to be obedient.

Practical Suggestions

- Recognise each of your children's gifts and abilities over and over again and thank God for them. Some talents are latent and will come out later and some appear as a result of an interest your child might have, which you have allowed him or her to pursue.

- Encourage your children to use their gifts and abilities to glorify God, help them to see when there are opportunities to do so and bless and encourage them when you've seen them doing just that. Encourage your children in attitudes of humility and a servant heart. Remind your children that our motivation for all we say or do comes out of a desire to serve and follow Jesus.

- Give your children the same degree of encouragement when they fail and help them to learn from their perceived 'failures.' As an example, a young boy we know missed two opportunities to pray out loud and to say something God had given him, both times in a large public setting, where most of the contributors were adults. The parents' response was:

First, they lifted all sense of guilt and bad feelings *('I failed Jesus')* from the child.

Second, they gave the child the truth to replace the sense of guilt: *'Actually, you just need more of Jesus in you to help you to speak out when he asks you to.'*

Third, the parents encouraged the boy to persevere and not give up, to ask Jesus to *'fill me and give me the courage to take hold of the new opportunities that will come.'*

Fourth, they gave the child more opportunities to preach at home, to seek God, to hear from God and to share it with the family in a small, intimate and non-threatening setting. This not only helped to develop his gift, but also gave him great encouragement: *'I am learning to appropriately share what I hear from God.'*

- Tell your children as many stories as possible of people you know who are finding their destiny in God. Do this as a direct encouragement to your children to find their own destiny. Always say, 'God has a wonderful, brilliant and amazing plan for you' to your child. It is the truth. Put up Jeremiah 29:11 in your home for a few weeks in a place where everyone will see it often. Encourage your own children's personal expectation of the wonderful things God has for them.

- Give unconditional approval, a sense of their worth and acceptance to your children. Thank God for their failures and turn those failures into opportunities for your children to experience your approval. Sometimes we, as parents, struggle with our children's failures, because they highlight our own weaknesses. We struggle to cope with our children especially if they fail to perform well publicly. It is often through our children experiencing parental approval in spite of and in the midst of failure, that they can learn to live with a sense of God's approval. When we live in approval, we are free to fail, free from an ungodly drive to please (to get it right) and free from unhealthy and intense self-examination which says, *'I should have'* out of a compelling drive to do 'what's right' or 'what pleases' the other person.

In order for our children to be able to use the gifts God has given them, they need *freedom from* and *freedom to*. They need freedom from ungodly drives, comparison and unhealthy desires. They need freedom to be themselves and to freely give of themselves and their talents.

It is also hard to give parental approval in the midst of discipline for unacceptable behaviour or attitudes. But this is when our children need our approval most, after they have failed and when they are 'in trouble'. They need to know that we still approve of them, though we disapprove of their behaviour.

- Make gift boxes with your children; they can be any colour or shape – alternatively they can be bought at card or gift shops. Use the boxes to make a note of the gifts you recognise that God has given to your children:

  - Personality gifts like: being a good friend, kindness, generosity, patience.
  - Spiritual gifts like: faith, self-control, wisdom, joy, peace.
  - Ability gifts like: sports, music, art, technical ability, entrepreneurial skill.

With your children, learn to celebrate God and thank him for the gifts he has given each of you. Help your children to understand that each of us is uniquely created and unlike anyone else; this is another reason to thank and bless God for how he has made you and me. Our purpose in helping our children to recognise their God-given talents, abilities and gifts should not be to give them licence to boast but rather to help our children to see themselves as God sees them. This ability will cover them and stand them in good stead in the battleground that is the school playground, where so many children are verbally abused by their peers.

The Body of Christ

How we as parents can mirror to our children Christ's own heart for his church in the midst of human failings, disappointments, discouragements and disillusionment. How we can model and inspire in our children not only a real love for the body of Christ but also practical ways of living and relating positively and radically as part of that body.

Within this chapter, we will also be discussing the all too little understood and less practised fact that we don't go to church – we ARE the church! In the light of this fact, how can we help and inspire our children to BE church 24 hours a day, seven days a week? We are the expression of Jesus on this earth, not just at a two-hour long meeting twice a week, but all the time.

We will also be distinguishing between those whose primary calling is to the body of Christ and those whose primary calling is to the world. By the body of Christ we mean those who already belong to and worship with a faith community of like-minded followers of Jesus. Some people are called to serve within the body of Christ. By the world we mean those who have never heard of Jesus, those who are at some stage of the way on a journey to faith, or those who may have little or no experience of a Christian faith community. They may never have attended a Christian meeting. Some people are called to serve Jesus in the world.

NOTE: We will use the phrase 'community of faith' in what follows, whenever we are speaking of what most people consider to be the church. For example, 'I attend the Methodist (or Catholic or Anglican) church.' When the word 'church' is used, we mean the universal church, which consists of everyone on earth who is a follower of Jesus.

Within the Community of Faith

'Do not neglect meeting together' (Hebrews 10:25, RSV). The fact is that wherever we live, the majority of people are outside the community of faith in which we feel comfortable, accepted and confident. Jesus' last words to his followers were to 'go into all the world and make disciples of all people'. It would seem that the people who are at the cutting edge of God's will in the earth are those who 'go out' from the community of faith 'into the world'. However, it is true of some churches that extra status is given to those who are perceived to have a public ministry to their own members. We desire to be like them, to have some form of public ministry ourselves so that we can receive similar status and worth. These mindsets are unhelpful and damaging.

The Bible teaches the opposite, rather that those who are prophets, teachers, pastors, etc., are servants of all rather than lords over all. They are there to equip and prepare God's people for their own ministries and 'works of service' in a hurting world. The sooner we realise that everyone has a wonderful calling and unique destiny in God and that he has created each of us with a purpose – the sooner we understand what God is asking of us, the sooner we will find peace and fulfilment and hear that 'Well done!' we so long for from the only One who matters. The truth is that most of us are called to the world, rather than to the community of faith and every

44

Christian is called to lead the way in his or her own sphere.

I have written much about relationships within the community of faith because Christians seem to have such difficulty in this area. We spend a great deal of time working through problems in the body of Christ, when I believe God's calling on the vast majority of Christians is to live the gospel in the world, so that true 'kingdom life' can permeate every level and aspect of the societies and cultures in which we live.

With all of the above in mind, I have tried to speak of difficulties within the community of faith for the sole purpose of challenging us all to begin to put aside our jealousies, our petty points of view and our frustrations with church politics. The aim is to challenge parents to:

- Desire to see the community of faith as Jesus sees it (I do not presume to 'have seen' this, but I do have a passion to understand Jesus' heart for his bride and what that means 'for me' in how I live my life);
- Grow up and mature in their dealings with other Christians;
- Find their destiny as the church in a world so full of pain and darkness; and
- Sacrifice a great and universal desire for a comfortable and middle-class life for the sake of those who are lost.

If only we could be at the place where the purpose of learning about godly relationships in the context of the local community of faith would be so that we could practise godly relationships, i.e. 'live' them in the world.

Leaders of children's groups can spend many hours teaching children about the body of Christ. However, it is in the home that children will surely learn the realities of the

Christian faith community their parents are involved in. The following points are key areas where we can influence our children. Depending on our own attitudes we could encourage our children to cultivate a love like Jesus has for the body of Christ. Alternatively we could cultivate a desire in our children to escape or withdraw from the hypocrisy and human failings they are exposed to. We need to be so careful, because despite what we preach, it is our own attitudes and actions that demonstrate to our children how we really live. Our children often copy what we demonstrate, they do what we do, not what we say. It is hoped that the following key points will serve at the very least as humble reminders to us all.

- The life and politics of any given community of faith can often be very sticky; we all have our pet problems, and have all been disillusioned on more than one occasion. Children have an amazing ability to pick up, as though they were created with an antenna for it, not only the minutest disgruntled comment we may make, but also the disgruntled or critical tone of voice we use when saying our piece. It can do no harm to remind and challenge all parents, guardians and leaders of our children's groups that Jesus died on a cross because of his undying love for his 'church'. We should do no less than to continually and in humility seek his heart for his church. Whatever is in our own hearts will surely have an influence on our children, despite what we say or how we appear on the surface.

- Related to the above, we cannot teach our children about unity in the body of Christ while we harbour any kind of criticism, hardheartedness or judgement of our community of faith or any of its members. We cannot teach our children how the body of Christ serves the world and each other, while we harbour resentments or hurts secretly or overtly. We dare not read our children the Scripture from John 13:34-35, 'Love one another. As I have loved you so you must love one another. By this everyone will know that you are my disciples, if you love one another' when we are not living this, from deep in our hearts. It is so important that our children do not hear us speaking critically or gossiping about our community of faith as an entity or about any individual member. We would totally undermine what we are trying to teach them, not to mention the harm those actions cause the whole body of Christ and the dishonour it would cause the One who died for us. On the contrary, it is so important that our children hear our sincere words when we speak well of our community of faith or when we verbally believe the best of all individuals within it whenever a relational difficulty arises.

- No community of faith is a building; every community of faith is made up of redeemed people. We don't go to church, we *are* the church! As a friend of mine called Gerald Coates often says: 'Most of us have no problem with our relationship with God; it's our relationships with his people that we can't cope with!' Jesus said the world would know we were his disciples – not by our ministries, or our miracles, or our theology or the numbers of people who come to our meetings, but by the love we have for one another (John 13:35). What a challenge! It is a hard fact that our children *will* follow in our footsteps. While it is unrealistic to think that we should never have a problem with anyone, how healthy for our kids to see us working through difficulties in love, commitment, faithfulness and humility.

What a worthwhile and profound lesson for them and what fruit will be produced in their lives as a result.

Example:

One family we know has gone through broken relationships in a particular community of faith, which seemed impossible to avoid. People on each side of the argument were hurt; everyone could truthfully say of those in the other camp, 'You have hurt me deeply.' Our friends soon began to realise that the only way forward was repentance and humility. They could only speak for themselves and could only respond to the Holy Spirit themselves. Someone said that when Jesus comes, he does not come to take sides but he comes to take over. Joshua found this when he met the captain of the armies of heaven and asked him whose side he was on. 'Are you for us or for our enemies?' (Joshua 5:13). The angel's reply was unequivocal, 'Neither [on your side or your enemy's], but as commander of the army of the Lord I have now come' (Joshua 5:14). So as our friends practised humility before the Lord, they began to realise that in the presence of his holiness and majesty, 'there is no one righteous, not even one' (Romans 3:10). They echoed the prayer of Isaiah when confronted with the Lord, 'Woe is me, for I am a person of unclean lips and I live in the midst of a people of unclean lips' (Isaiah 6:5). So they laid it all at the cross. They laid down their hurt, the offence they felt, their desire for vindication, their perception that they were more 'right' than the other group. They laid it all at the cross and left it there. It was hard and it took a bit of time but it was a choice. They chose not to rely on their own understanding of the situation. They let go of all these attitudes and cried out to God for mercy, mercy for themselves and mercy for everyone who had been involved. Today, there is no pain and the memories are dimmed; many of the relationships have been restored. In fact, when at a party recently, the family were amazed to meet up with at least five or six families they had been in broken relationship with. They were astounded to find that there was only joy in being together. And the family has been able to continue in heartfelt prayer for many others they have not seen again. They have been a demonstration to us that we can love one another.

- As Christians we all know we are not perfect, we are redeemed. Most faith communities are full of people who have made big mistakes in their dealings with one another. There is a great temptation for most of us who have spent a number of years within the same community of faith to begin to take for granted some of the very things that inspired us when we first joined. Ways of doing things get a bit tiresome and we lose our initial sense of appreciation for some of the people we now know only too well. We can lose our initial sense of joy in corporate worship and we can become too blasé about our times of ministry to one another. These attitudes will surely pass on to our children. There is a challenge to us to look with new eyes at the specific Christian community we are so sure the Lord has put us in. (If we are in the wrong community of faith, then why have we not moved on to where we know we should be?) We can sincerely pray for God to give us his perspectives in every aspect of faith community family life. We can also pray sincerely for God's mercy on our own faith community and for the freshness of his Spirit to blow through it, bringing his life. It's not 'God have mercy on this community, they have some real problems' but rather

'God have mercy on *us,* and that includes me! – I am part of this faith community.'

- Wherever and whenever possible, let's express with our children our gratitude to God for the church and for our own community of faith. Express it in prayer, in discussion and in acts of kindness and thanksgiving. Let's thank God often for the people, for the practices we appreciate and for the blessings we have received. Let's lead our children in loving the body of Christ.

- All of the above is not to blindly ignore some of the real problems within communities of faith, which do exist and which do need solving. How many of us can say, however, that we have actually spent time in the presence of Jesus interceding over those problems and hearing from the Lord how we can help to bring his solution or his way through. Sometimes the Lord doesn't tell us the solution, sometimes we are simply asked to pray. To pray with sincerity, humility and with a pure heart can be the most difficult challenge of all.

Often, the Lord asks us to walk *through* difficulties with others we would not naturally gravitate towards, another challenge. It does no good for us to wash our hands of the body of Christ and to go it alone. Many of Paul's writings focus on relationships, attitudes and ways of doing things within the community of faith, suggesting the importance of that community for all people. God has a clear stated purpose and agenda for the whole church, as expressed in much of the New Testament.

The World – Locally, Nationally and Beyond

Some people are called to serve the body of Christ within a specific congregation or community of faith. They have a real ministry to teach or care for or serve the individual people who identify with their congregation. Some people are called to *be* the body of Christ and even to serve the body of Christ beyond the congregation. Others are called to be a bridge between the two.

We often have such strong mindsets of what being church means, what shape it is or must be, how it works, who is allowed to belong and when, what is acceptable and what is not. We forget that Jesus asked us to make disciples of *'all people'*. 'All people' are rarely found within the community of faith we are part of and worship with. 'All people' are found in the world, where we also live over 95 per cent of our time. They are found in the school, the office, the job or next door. They are even found in other communities of faith we relate with or work with or attend school with.

Our challenge is to be able to carry the presence of Jesus wherever we go, to speak, act, think, relate, work in a way that reflects his kingdom, his goodness, his power and his life. Wow!

Our challenge is to change clothes. We can wear as a protective covering our fear of the heathen, dark, dangerous world. This fear alienates us from the hurts and hardness we see all around. Instead we need to clothe ourselves with the compassion of Jesus, which will be both a real source of protection for us, and a real source of hope for those in such great need, those whom we find around every corner. I know of no better way to rid ourselves of the fear of this bad old world, than to be immersed in and covered by the Lord's perfect love.

Our challenge is to not be afraid to link with other communities of faith for the sake of a certain territory or geography. For instance, we know a group of people who are part of one faith community but are working with many other Christians from other faith communities to be a presence in the local hospital in the area where they live. They all have the same heart for the sick, and are working and praying together to achieve the same goals. They all feel God is asking similar things of them and they need to link together and in humility serve each other to achieve God's purposes. They have not started their own 'church', they all still belong to their respective faith communities, but they work and pray together when it comes to relating to people in hospital.

Our Children

Our attitudes towards our community of faith and towards the church in general, our behaviour, our fears, our words, our struggles, all these serve as a window through which our children will form a mindset about the body of Christ. *God help us to live in such a way that our children can see through that window clearly, and can see God's heart for the body of Christ.* Please may our children never see that window masked over by our prejudices, our disappointments, our bitterness or our pain. Please God, let our children see our glorious purpose as the body of Christ. Help them to understand through us, that we are Jesus' hands and feet in this world. May our children see their parents actively 'being' salt and light in their local community, may they see us as ministers of reconciliation and using our God-given gifts everywhere we go.

- Children love to copy their parents. So wherever we serve in the community of faith, or in our neighbourhood, we can include our children. They can serve right alongside us. No task should be 'beneath' our station or self-perceived status. We can impart so much to our children while we serve. Through whatever jobs we do, we can do our very best, 'as to the Lord' (Colossians 3:17, 23) and can be a blessing to others. Our young children will copy us. These will be the foundations laid in their young lives, which we can build on as they grow older.

Example:

One family we know lived next door to an 80-year-old widow, who had lost her husband in the past five years and who lived alone. They began to treat the lady as part of their family, including her in birthdays and Christmas celebrations. They shared plants and flowers with each other, and the children treated her a little like a grandma. The lady accompanied them to school concerts and they talked about their lives together. Even though the lady had a strong negative mindset about Christians, the opportunity did arise for the family to share their faith, and to speak frankly with their neighbour about knowing Jesus. She listened and spoke with them about Jesus because she and the family were friends, she belonged with them, she was comfortable with them and she knew they loved her.

- We can recognise the gifts God has given our children and look to see how each gift can be used within our own faith community. Is it to pray? To worship? To speak about Jesus? Or how each gift can be used in their sphere of influence at school or at a club. Is it a gift of friendship? Is it peacemaking? Is it acceptance of others?

- Ideally, it would be wonderful if all faith communities recognised and esteemed the ministry of children in the same way that they recognise and esteem the ministry of adults. We are all at different places in our understanding of God's heart for all generations within the body of

Christ where we worship. We would encourage you to go as far as you can in your own faith community. If adults in your faith community feel uncomfortable with children in the prayer group, or if adults cannot understand that children can receive important words from God, then why not have a group of children to your home? Why not teach them to pray, right alongside your own children?

- 'Youth with a Mission' have something called Daniel Prayer Groups, which can be a great help to parents who would like to start something similar. Resources are available, through YWAM, to help those adults who would like to mentor praying children.

- Encourage your children to hear from God and to worship and to pray, both while in a Christian gathering and at home, while on an errand or on a walk. Don't wait for Sundays to pray with your children, to read the Bible with them, to listen to God, to worship, to have times of repentance and forgiveness together. It's a lame excuse to say, 'I lead a busy life; I don't have time for all this.' We all have time for aggressive behaviour, we have the time to hurt one another in word and deed; we say it's all part of daily life. Then we must also have time to be reconciled together, and time for repentance and forgiveness.

- Respect and act upon the things the Lord has spoken to your children about. If he gives them a word for your faith community, which you believe to be relevant and which you believe to be from God, then stand with your children and help them to appropriately deliver that word.

- If your children hear from God some words or direction about being the church in the local community or if your children feel that some action needs to be taken (for example to visit someone, to give something away, to do something to encourage someone), then stand with your children. Go and do the specific action with them.

- Be open to teaching your children about different expressions of the body of Christ in different nations and together learn to respect and appreciate the unique ways other Christians express and live out their faith.

For example:

- The way many Africans name their children, giving them names that have great significance in terms of their meaning and therefore represent the parents' hope for their children (e.g. names like 'God saves me', 'the Lord is my Rock', and so on).

- The devoutness of some Christian faith communities; for example, I was in the Catholic Church for the first ten years of my life and I have never forgotten the wonderful devotion to God that I learned there.

- The great generosity of some third world Christian faith communities.

- The different ways of worship.

The Love of God
Ways to express unconditional love for your children.

- Give continual approval no matter what the behaviour; we can discipline children and be very clear about behaviour that is unacceptable, but whereas people often withdraw approval for bad behaviour God never does. Unless, as parents, we ourselves know the unconditional approval and love of God in our everyday lives it will be nearly impossible to give it to our children.

- We need to give our children the freedom to fail; getting *through* failure in society's terms will often equal success in God's terms. Sometimes we as parents cannot allow our children to fail publicly because it hurts our own pride and we become ashamed of our own children. Sometimes we put our own extreme competitiveness onto our children and expect them to behave in the same way. We need to remember that our children, though they inherit many tendencies from us, are also individuals and may be totally unlike us in other respects.

Example:

Many of us have probably been to a school sports tournament, or a kids' sports club, where we've witnessed a parent loudly coaching their child from the sidelines. Sometimes we've witnessed a parent yelling at their child to do better; first in an encouraging manner and later on even in an abusive way. I will never forget the friend who could not allow her daughter to play an after-school game without shouting instructions as to how to play. It was embarrassing for the rest of the onlookers and was unhelpful and discouraging for the child.

- Look at 1 Corinthians 13 and ask for God's help in loving your child with that kind of love. Really rejoice in problems, troubles and difficulties and look at them as opportunities to practise godly love rather than as obstacles to family harmony.

- Ask for God's help in treating your child with the respect, honour and courtesy he or she needs and which *every* person should receive.

- Related to the above is that, in the kingdom of God, children stand side by side and shoulder to shoulder with every other Christian, in terms of their potential anointing, their ability to relate to God and the way they should be treated. The Bible teaches us to honour (Romans 12:10), prefer (Philippians 2:3), serve (Galatians 5:13; 6:2) and respect (1 Peter 2:17) one another. As parents, we can be leading the way in recognising our children and youth as God recognises them. David Walters, author of a book called *Kids in Combat: Training children and youth to be powerful for God,* often comments, 'Children do not have a junior Holy Spirit . . .' Wes Campbell, pastor of a church in Western Canada, says that children are not little lambs in the kingdom, but little sheep and Jesus said that his sheep listen to his voice (John 10).

- Make repentance and forgiveness a normal part of family life, in which parents are on the same level as everyone else and not above everyone else. Sometimes parents put themselves on a level where they never admit their own mistakes, wrongdoings or failures. Children see our faults; to hide them is only deceiving everyone and can not only cause damage and cynicism in children's lives but can cause our children to copy us. How sad when, because of us, our children struggle with their own mistakes and failures or, worse still, try to hide them? God's way is for openness, repentance and forgiveness, no matter what our age, our job, our function or our status in society.

- Keep short accounts with God when you fail to show your children unconditional love. Yield again to his mercy and work in your life and receive his grace to cover your own mistakes. Never be afraid to admit to your children when you are wrong.

- Find countless ways to express your love for your children, not when they do something good or clever, but because of who they are. What do you love about your child? Does he or she know how you feel?

- Spend time with your children on a one-to-one basis. Have 'dates', where Mum or Dad spends a few hours with each child, once every few months. Go for walks, go for ice cream, go swimming or ice-skating, go shopping or rowing, go on a bike ride or a picnic together. Take the time to invest in your relationship with your children.

- When your child finishes last or does badly in a school play or sports day, show great approval and give your warm congratulations 'for doing your best!'

- A wonderful book, which contains 365 ways to tell your child 'I Love You', is called *Faith Training* (by Joe White, published by Tyndale House, 1996). Following are a few samples:

  - When your child is participating in an athletic event or musical performance, be there watching. (p. 111)

  - Walk in the rain and jump puddles together. (p. 112)

  - Sit down together and watch your child's favourite TV show. (p. 112)

  - Prepare your child's favourite dinner menu twice in one week. (p. 112)

  - The Bible's love chapter says that love is 'patient' (1 Corinthians 13:4). Have you recently failed to be patient in some way with your child? If so, confess that failure to God and ask (and expect) his help in overcoming impatience. Obey his Spirit's prompting whenever he reminds you not to be so uptight and demanding. (p. 113)

  - Make cookies together; then put them on neighbours' doorsteps, ring the doorbell, and run. (p. 114)

  - When you sense something is troubling your child, make a reason for a trip in the car alone together. (p. 115)

  - Ask for your child's opinion on a big family decision. (p. 116)

  - Never say 'I'm too busy.' (p. 116)

  - The Bible's love chapter says that love 'keeps no record of wrongs' (1 Corinthians 13:5). Have you learned to let go of your child's past failures? (p. 117)

– Take your child out to breakfast (just the two of you) before school. (p. 117)

– Allow your child to plan the day for your family. (p. 117)

– When your child is upset or hurt, make listening your first response. (p. 119)

– Talk about what you believe about God. (p. 117)

– Share your life with your child; let him or her into your world. Tell him or her the things you like most about your life and work, and talk together about some of the frustrations as well. Talk about your hopes and dreams in every area of your life. (p. 120)

– Talk frequently with your child about the truths in the Bible that you're enjoying in reading and meditation. (p. 122)

– Tell your child how you most want to improve in your life in the coming year, and ask him or her to pray for you. (p. 123)

– Invite your child's friends over, build a mountain on a tray out of ice cream scoops and whipped cream (with all the toppings), and then eat it. (p. 125)

– Start praying now for the spouses your children will have someday. Pray that their marriages will be strong and Christ-centred. (p. 127)

– Take advice from your kids and encourage them to give it freely, even when it is confronting and personal. (p. 127)

Giving – God is Generous

Helping our children to grow in their understanding of the generous heart of God the Father towards his beloved children. Helping our children to see God's generosity towards them. Also helping our children to grow in their own ability to give joyfully to God and to others out of their own heart response to God. Giving is defined as giving time to others, giving money, giving our prayers, giving our service, giving practical help or counselling, giving encouragement or giving away a possession.

As parents and carers, we all need to open our own hearts before God with regards to our attitudes towards giving. Is there something he wants to adjust in us, before we speak as though we 'know it all' about giving?

- Practise naming together with your children, at least once per week, 'What has God done for me, for our family this past week or past few days?' Thank God together.

- Practise thanking God with your children not for what he has done for you, but for who he is: for his presence, his forgiveness, his love, and his greatness, his holiness, his mercy, his kindness. Thank him for his Son and for

Jesus' life, for Jesus' death, for Jesus' resurrection and for Jesus' love. Thank him for the Holy Spirit and for who he is. Read the Bible with your children and speak out Scriptures that exalt or magnify or glorify God, as Father, as Son and as Holy Spirit.

- Ask God together to take you on as a family, to help you to grow in your own ability to give and ask God to give you his generous heart.

- Learn as a family and learn by practice, to give out of a response to God the Holy Spirit and not out of guilt or other ungodly motivation. Tell your children when God is speaking to you about giving time, friendship, material things, money or practical help. Help your children to see opportunities to give of their time or money or practical help or friendship. Encourage them to hear from God so that their giving can be a response to him. Teach your children by experience that giving out of a response to God is a joy even though it may be costly. Alternatively, they may learn from experience that giving out of guilt is a burden and heaviness, whatever it costs.

Example:

A boy we know was pressured into feeling guilty because he was not giving of his time like others were to get a certain venture going in his church. His parents used the opportunity to help him to understand that he should give out of a heart response to God and never because of what others were doing or because of their expectations of him. Again, we need to learn so that we can teach our children, that there is one person and one person only we are to live to please. That is the Lord Jesus. It does not matter what others think of us, if we are humbling ourselves before the Lord and being obedient to him.

- The Bible speaks about attitudes towards giving (2 Corinthians 9:7). Practise with your children good attitudes toward giving. For example, doing the washing-up cheerfully and without complaining can be an exercise for all the family in giving in the home. This is a good example of just practising a giving heart in the midst of everyday life experiences. *Give* your children positive encouragement when they display a giving heart, or when they give with a cheerful attitude.

- Share wonderful stories with your children – stories of how others have given, sometimes with great sacrifice and how God has provided for them. Share these stories to build your children's faith.

  Example:

  We know a family who have been in very difficult financial position for many years. Yet their home is always open to needy people and they always share what they have. Each Christmas, on 25 December their children choose one of their favourite toys and take it to a local hospital and give it to some children there. Needless to say, this family has experienced miraculous provision from God – they have had money put through their door, food left on their doorstep, school places opened up to their children, and jobs for both parents.

- Practise giving of your finances, whatever your financial situation, and don't hide it from your children. Encourage your children to give out of the money they receive as well. Learn what the Bible has to say about giving of the first fruits of all that we earn. Learn and understand what your faith community teaches about tithing.

Example:

Once, as a family, we found ourselves looking forward to some money we knew we'd be receiving out of an insurance policy. We planned what we'd do with the money. Then the Lord spoke to us and asked us to give it all away to a worthwhile cause. As parents we felt we should obey and we talked it through with our children. They agreed but then we did this: We bought the largest bag of rice we could find. We sat each of our children on a chair with a bowl in their lap, one at a time. We read the Scripture, 'Give and it will be given to you. A good measure, pressed down, shaken together and running over, will be poured into your lap. For with the measure you use, it will be measured to you' Luke 6:38. As we read we explained to the children that this is what our Father God is like; we had such a sense that all heaven was near. We gave them each a turn then and poured the rice into their bowl, letting it over-flow onto their laps and even onto the floor. 'This is what God is like!' we exclaimed. This is his heart when we give, especially out of obedience! We had a wonderful time together laughing and praying, committing ourselves afresh to God's purposes. Our eldest son really got into the moment, grabbing handfuls of rice and pouring them over our youngest son's head. The conclusion of this story is that within months, we received many times over what we had sacrificially given away.

I believe that everything I have belongs to God, therefore how is he leading me to use all the money, time, energy and skill he has given me? I do not believe that just 10 per cent of what I earn or have should be 'tithed' to God and the rest is up to me to use as I please. The Bible says, in a number of different ways, that all things exist for Jesus and I believe that includes everything I am and everything I have:

- Romans 11:36 (International Standard Version) 'For all things are from him, by him and for him.'
- Colossians 1:16 (King James Version) 'All things were created by him and for him.'
- Hebrews 2:10 (American Standard Version) 'For it became him, for whom are all things . . .'

• Make giving into a family practice. One never has too little to give something. The Bible says, 'Out of his fullness, we have all received' (John 1:16), and God's fullness is awesome! If we can live our lives immersed in the love of God, we can always give something with a cheerful heart whatever our material situation. A thankful heart finds being a blessing to others as natural as breathing. True giving, which echoes the Father's heart, is a heart attitude, which any actions then flow out of. Giving is not just money; it is equally important to give time, encouragement, friendship, help and support. And our children can be a part of all of this. They can walk the whole journey with us, they can learn by our example to rejoice whether we have little or nothing. They can learn right alongside us to experience God's generous heart.

• So let's also listen when our children hear from God and feel that they need to give a specific something away. The following example illustrates that, out of life situations, we can also teach our children about sacrificial giving and even allow them to experience it.

Example:

We remember a time when our daughter had received a talking dolly when she was about four. The dolly was very expensive for us to buy and we hoped she'd keep it for years. She didn't seem to play with it all that much, though she really loved it. A year later she said, 'I want to give this dolly away.' She wanted to give her dolly to an older girl whose parents were both unemployed and who could not afford Christmas gifts. We could have said, 'You can't give the dolly away, it cost us too much!' We could have thought, 'She can't know what she is doing, she is just a child.' We could have forbidden her to give it away; in our parental wisdom, we actually felt the day might come when she would miss it. We talked with her about some of the implications and she was still adamant she needed to give it away. So she did and it was a great blessing to another child. Sure enough, five years or so later, she told us that she had missed her dolly every now and again, and realised as she got older that she had given away something which was very precious to her.

We were able to talk with her again about sacrificial giving, that giving which actually costs us something, not just giving away our unwanted items, but at times giving things which are precious to us. It was a great and lasting lesson for all of us. And yes, the Lord has richly blessed our daughter and she has no regret today.

Holy and Anointed One

Praising Jesus in the home is natural and rewarding. The following practical suggestions not only help parents to teach praise as a way of life, but to cultivate in their children attitudes of thankfulness and worship in contexts of creativity, fun and freedom.

- Take some worship songs, which lend themselves to creative expression, and act them out at home with your children. For example, in the song 'Holy and Anointed One' by John Barnett (1989, Vineyard Ministries International):

  1. The songwriter speaks of Jesus' name being like honey on our lips. Give your children a taste of honey and talk with them about what honey tastes like and explain how that is what the psalm writer felt about even the mention of Jesus' name.

  2. He speaks of the Spirit being like water to our souls. Give your children a drink of cold water on a hot day and again, talk about how it feels. Use words like 'refreshing' or 'invigorating' and then explain that the Holy Spirit is like this.

  3. He quotes Psalm 119:105 saying, 'Your word is a lamp unto my feet'. When it is dark outside see if your children

can negotiate a path around some obstacles when all the lights are turned off inside your house. Then use a torch and discuss what effect the light has. Then discuss with your children why the psalm writer uses this analogy.

Following are some other examples, which are meant not only to be copied, but to inspire each reader's creative use of worship songs which are precious to you. It is the author's firm belief that each of us can tap into the Lord's infinite creativity and receive inspiration direct from him. This ability to receive inspiration from God can be developed, just as we develop other skills, through practice and regular use.

– 'I Walk by Faith' by Chris Falson (1991, Seam of Gold): Walk back and forth with your children in time to the music. Literally walk by faith! This is not just a little game we can play with our children to humour them or even to help them engage with worship. This can become a powerful prophetic enactment as well as a clear statement of how you want to live your life. Then the Lord lends his support and his power to help you to do so. From personal experience in our own family and in the families of many friends, we have realised that God takes these times seriously.

Example:

We have been amazed by the results of our prophetic enactment of this song alone. Over the years, we have learned about faith, we have become a family that lives by faith, and is learning to live more by faith, and our faith has grown and grown.

– Watch children's worship videos with your children and participate! Dance and do the actions together.

- 'The River is Here' by Andy Park (1994, Mercy Vineyard Publishing) or 'Find Me in the River' by Martin Smith (Furious Music UK). Get these tapes and play them to your children, teach your children these songs and use them in your family worship.

- Get a long piece of blue cloth (you could use an old sheet), wave it up and down in your home. (You could have two adults standing some metres apart each holding two corners or ends of the sheet.) Let the children jump about in your 'river of God'. Lift the river up and let the children go under it to symbolise getting immersed in the river (see Ezekiel 47). Have your children simply lay on the river as you play a worship song (examples above). Describe the benefits of the river of God. See the book *The River of God* by Dutch Sheets, and read his vision of being in the river of God (p. 9) even to children as young as 5 or 6. Encourage your children to draw pictures of the river of God. Worship with your children.

Example:

We have had profound and wonderful times in our own home through using a simple piece of blue cloth. The presence of God has come into our home, we have rested in his presence, we have seen visions, received strength and inspiration, and just experienced his amazing love.

- 'He Brought Me to His Banqueting Table' by Kevin Prosch (1991, Thankyou Music). Make banners with your children and wave them over one another while you play the tape or CD and sing this song together. You can write Bible verses about God's love on the banners.

- Help your children to learn your faith community's current popular songs. Teach your children the words to the songs and explain the meanings. This will help the children to feel part of and to participate in corporate worship. Use ribbons, banners, flags and musical instruments often at home.

- Play worship music often in the home. Realise that worship actually has a significant effect on the spiritual atmosphere in a physical place. Use worship music to fill your home with the presence of Jesus.

- Learn the power of thanksgiving. Fill your home with thanksgiving. Learn to see God's blessings in your life and in your family life. Teach your children to express thanksgiving and to acknowledge God's hand in their lives. We are not talking about mindless legalistic 'prayers of thanks', repeated day in and day out, but rather creative and joyful expressions of sincere and heartfelt gratitude to God out of supernatural revelation of what he has done and who he is in our lives. Thank God in all situations (Ephesians 1:16; 5:20).

Example:

We were under a time of intense spiritual attack as a family; life was hard and uncertain. We deliberately had a feast one evening, making a wonderful meal of favourite foods and reading Psalm 23: 'He lays a table before me in the presence of my enemies.' We wanted to physically experience what that felt like; we thanked God together for the reality of his presence through our hard time. It felt like a very significant meal that evening. In general, though, many of us are not always fully aware of the spiritual repercussions of our temporal actions. We walk by faith and not by sight, so we had our feast in faith. We believed in the goodness of God and were prepared to make a practical statement of that belief.

• Here are a few examples of the countless ways we can express thanksgiving to God. We don't have to always sit down, fold hands, or even sit still to have a thankful heart or to express our thanks in words:

  – in the middle of family times of worship (for life, love, health, his presence),

  – on a walk (for nature, for legs that work!),

  – after an exam (for his help in making it through),

  – in sickness (for his touch and his promises regarding healing) and health,

  – while shopping (for provision),

  – before eating (for the ability to enjoy such abundance and for his provision),

  – during a sports event (for protecting a hurt player from serious injury).

There is a power released in the midst of God's people expressing thanks, which we may not fully understand. So be truly thankful and teach your children to be thankful.

• With your children, explore the following ideas:

  – Art is worship or art as worship;

  – Art is prayer or art as prayer.

Learn with your children, to express prayer and worship through art. There are literally endless ways of doing this, ways that are inspired by the Master Artist himself. Following are a few very simple examples to help the reader to understand what we are getting at. Our aim is to challenge parents and all those involved with children to receive creative inspiration from God the Holy Spirit.

Example:

A young teenage girl we know has a heart for children at risk both here and abroad. She was at a Christian based art event, where the participants were encouraged to merge their art with worship. So the girl made the most amazing painting to depict the hopelessness and pain and brokenness which many children experience, and then immersed the images of pain in a depiction of the river of God. I have no doubt that her art was both worship and intercession, in other words, intercessory worship.

- Use a long piece of wallpaper lining paper. Lay it down across the living room floor or put it across the wall in a long, well-lit hallway. Over the next few days, encourage family members to draw on it. Encourage one another to picture their prayers, as we can sometimes express what God shows us more easily through pictures than through words. Pictures can also sometimes express what words cannot.

Example:

One evening we got together with an intergenerational group of young people aged 9-17. We decided to bless the Lord. We laid out the wallpaper and coloured pens and then we put on a worship tape. Everyone was encouraged to write or draw something to express the wonder, the goodness, the love, the majesty of God. There were to be no requests written down. We just wanted to express something that would touch the Lord's heart. The results were astounding! Children came up with amazing insights into the beauty of the Lord's character and his goodness in his relationship with us. They came up with insight as to the Lord's feelings for us too. And the room was filled with his sweet presence.

- Develop your own ability to worship. Let God explode away your mindsets of what worship is. Share what you are learning with your children and teach them to worship by doing it with them.

- We may also need a touch from God to enable us to worship in freedom, sometimes especially in our own homes in front of our own family. Children do not have to copy their parents' style of worship, though they may begin that way.

- Let's be open to learn new styles of worship from our children. Let *us* – mature adults – be the ones who are flexible and open to change, rather than always expecting our children or young people to comply with what we find comfortable. May God save us from an attitude of 'If you don't do it the way I do, it's not true worship.' The truth is that though we may have absolutely wonderful ways of worship, our way is not the only way.

- Linked with the above is the challenging and inspiring idea that we can actually *be* worship. An act of compassion, a kind word, a choice to forgive someone, even the degree to which we open our hearts to God – all these things and more – can be classed as worship. Darlene Zschech of Hillsongs expresses this very well in her song, 'Shout to the Lord' (1993). The songwriter expresses her deep desire that we never cease to worship the Lord through our every breath and through all that we are.

- Let's lead our children in remembering the object of our worship, which is not a sense of comfort or familiarity, or a pleasant or exhilarating feeling – it is Jesus our Saviour – the Mighty and Awesome One and Only –

Glorious and Holy – King of the Nations! We are challenged to remember with humility that our primary focus of worship is not a method; it is Jesus!

• Help your children to learn to worship Jesus for who he is rather than for what he can do for them. There is a place in the presence of Jesus where nothing else matters. He is everything – he fills everything – and his presence is at once everything we desire. There is certainly a time for asking Jesus to do things for us, Jesus himself taught us to do so. The church doesn't have difficulty in asking Jesus for provision, for blessing, for healing, for prosperity. And yet, please God, help the church to come back to her first love, to that place where she is enraptured simply by – the face of Jesus – who he is, his beauty, his nature, his heart. We can do no better than to cultivate this one desire in our children – which is greater than all the other noble and godly desires in Christianity put together – to pursue the presence of Jesus with every ounce of their being. Our children can have no higher goal or calling in their whole lives than to worship and adore at the feet of Jesus Christ. It is my firm belief that visions and dreams and a connection with 'what you and I were born for' comes from this place of simply being with the Lord. It is from here that we can receive the Lord's instructions and commissioning for today, for the next year or for our whole life.

These are days of corruption in politics, sin in the church, hypocrisy and unrighteousness in business, broken homes, unprecedented media influence, hopelessness and rebellion in schools, and a massively increased interest in the supernatural. In these days our children are both in great danger and in great need. It is sad but true that a watered down, comfortable, compromising and materialistic faith will not satisfy the need of the emerging generations. It will not compete with the colour, the excitement, the get-rich-quick schemes and the instant gratification, which tempts them from every direction.

Our children are in need of the same fiery and unquenchable faith that sustained thousands of brave hearts through the ages, who did not love their lives as much as to shrink from death (Revelation 12:11). When the pursuit of the presence of Jesus becomes our greatest goal, highest joy and only reward, only then will we have a real and effective alternative in the fierce battle that is constantly raging over the minds and hearts of our children.

May God help us to remember the first commandment and desire to 'love the Lord your God with all your heart and with all your soul and with all your mind' (Matthew 22:37). My fervent prayer is that our children can see in the older generation in these days a pure and insatiable passion for Jesus.

The Name of Jesus

Through day-by-day exposure to Jesus, by speaking and learning about each and every name the Bible gives to him, day after day, year after year, we will help our children to learn about our Saviour. By walking through the situations of life with your children and hand in hand with the 'Good Shepherd' or the 'Lion of the Tribe of Judah', we can help our children to know Jesus as their personal friend and Saviour.

- Pray at home in Jesus' name and encourage your children to do the same. (I'll never forget the true story of the child of some friends, who was very young and had been left on the upstairs toilet while Mum and Dad were welcoming in some visitors. 'In Jesus' name, get me off this loo!' came the commanding shout from somewhere above. Not quite what we had in mind.)

- Explore with your children all the names given to Jesus and what they mean. Help your children to understand different facets of Jesus' amazing character. Take time to meditate on the facets of Jesus' character as embodied in each of the names given to him. Teach your children what it means to meditate. *The Oxford Popular Dictionary* gives lots of helpful hints: 'To be lost in thought, to consider, contemplate, deliberate, mull things over, muse, ponder, pray, reflect, think deeply.' Thank Jesus together that he is the Lord of lords, or the Bright and Morning Star. Declare out his names as you worship with your children. Some of the names are as follows:

Son of God – Matthew 8:29

The King of Israel – John 12:13

The Gate for the Sheep – John 7:9

The True Vine – John 15:1

The True Light (who gives light to everyone) – John 1:9

Lord of Lords – Revelation 19:17

Son of Man – Matthew 9:6

Lord – Matthew 8:2

Faithful and True – Revelation 19:11

The Resurrection and the Life – John 11:25

The Alpha and Omega – Revelation 17:8

The Good Shepherd – John 10:14

Immanuel – Isaiah 7:14; Matthew 1:23

The Root and Offspring of David; The Bright and Morning Star! – Revelation 22:16

The Word – John 1:1

Master – Luke 9:49

The Head of the Church – Ephesians 5:23

The Christ, the son of the Living God – Matthew 16:16

The Prophet – Matthew 21:11

King of Kings – Revelation 19:17

The Way, the Truth and the Life – John 14:6

Saviour – Luke 2:11

God's One and Only Son – John 3:16

The Bread of Life – John 6:35

The King of the Jews – Matthew 27:11

The Lamb of God – who takes away the sin of the world – John 1:29

Wonderful, Counsellor, the Mighty God, the Everlasting Father, the Prince of Peace – Isaiah 9:6

The King – Matthew 25:39

Son of David – Matthew 20:30

Teacher – Matthew 22:16

The Great High Priest – Hebrews 4:8

The Bridegroom – Revelation 21:9; Ephesians 5:25-33

The Lion of the Tribe of Judah – Revelation 5:5

Faithful and True – Revelation 19:11

- Read Acts 3:1-10 with your children and explain that we can pray for people in Jesus' name. Encourage your children to begin in small ways, by praying for a neighbour with a cold or praying for a sick friend at school. Learning to pray in the name of Jesus is a lifelong process, so share with your children as you learn. Share your own experiences of praying 'in Jesus' name'.

- Teach your children to listen to Jesus and respond to him, as he constantly responded to his father: *I only do what I see my Father doing.* In one sense, we can pray in Jesus' name all the time. There are other occasions as we respond to the prompting of the Holy Spirit, especially when we are praying for healing or deliverance, where praying in Jesus' name will have dramatic and dynamic results because our prayers are a direct response to what God wants to do. Help your children to understand that not everyone who is sick, for example, gets healed. This shouldn't stop us praying for anyone who is sick, especially as we are praying in our own homes. Let's learn to hear from God and to recognise when he is putting someone on our heart and calling us to pray for them. Let's lead our children in practising perseverance. We live in a quick-fix society, when things need to happen instantly – when we search incessantly for instant gratification. Because of this conditioning, our children can become discouraged when the person they are praying for isn't instantly healed. These times are opportunities for us as parents to model to our children perseverance, faithfulness, patience and a trust in God 'for as long as it takes'.

• If Jesus speaks to our children about a situation, we need to be ready to yield to God and pray with our child with all our hearts even if we don't have faith for supernatural intervention in that situation. We need to be instruments of blessing. 'No, Mrs Smith will probably never get well', is a negative comment and our tongues are powerful instruments to bring real blessing or cursing into the lives of others. We need to encourage our child's faith and what they have heard from God. Let's not pour cold water on them every time they feel God has spoken to them. (*No, son, Jesus is not going to give you a pet – it won't happen unless I buy one and I'm not going to.*) In our situation, we supported our 3-year-old child's belief that God was going to give him a pet and stood with him in his prayers even though we weren't keen and didn't think his prayers would be answered.

About three weeks later, suddenly and with no warning, we were given a rabbit, complete with hutch and dish!

So let's support our children with humility as they learn to walk with God. We may find that our children may hear from God more clearly than we ourselves do. Let's thank God and let's be open to not only learning from our children but also open to receiving prayer from them.

Christmas with or without Jesus
Helping our children to find the reason
behind the season.

There is always a challenge to parents at Christmas time, when many are torn between their natural desire to give wonderful gifts to their children and their dislike of the materialism that has gripped nearly everything associated with Christmas. To find new and creative ways to help our children to focus on Jesus at Christmas time is a great and worthwhile challenge. Additionally, why don't we live in some of the positive spirit we find at Christmas, all year round? Why should we focus on Jesus, on giving, on joy and celebration just at Christmas time? This is perhaps the greatest challenge to us.

- Continue to find new and creative ways of family worship. Christmas often gives us opportunities to turn our worship outwards, with events such as carol singing times around the neighbourhood. In these times, why not turn the tables and *give* treats or home-made goodies to the neighbours, who will often be expecting you to be collecting money? Why not let God's wonderful gift of his Son challenge you in August or May to find ways to turn worship and celebration outward and share Jesus with the neighbours?

- Help your children to focus on giving rather than on receiving; what can we as a family give during this season in terms of time, friendship, food, service? How can we bring God's kingdom in a relevant and radical way into our 'bit' of neighbourhood, job and school during this season? How can we carry on all year round?

- There is a revival song, called 'Enemy's Camp' by Richard Black, which has been popular in Brownsville, Pensacola, USA. It is all about taking back what we have been robbed of.

Let's take Christmas back from the control of the spirit of this age and use the season as a celebration of God's love and the gift of his amazing Son for me, for my family and for all humanity. We do not want to ban the trees, traditions and tinsel from our celebrations of Christmas, but let's teach our children by our own lifestyle, that they are very much our secondary focus; the primary purpose of Christmas is a celebration of Jesus.

- Let us focus with our children on some of the fruit of knowing Jesus: friendship, relationship and family.

- Following are some radical expressions of Christmas, which real people have practised over the past few years:

  - A couple who have no children of their own spend about seven days over Christmas week (when they both have time off from their regular jobs) working at an inner city shelter for the homeless. Christmas dinner is provided for homeless people, along with beds, toiletries, warm gloves and coats and three meals each day for the week. The couple work the night shift and have their own Christmas dinner with friends just before they go to work.

– A 16-year-old friend last Christmas said to her mum: *Whatever money you were going to spend on me this Christmas, please take it and give it away* (she named a charity for the poor in her town). The mother said this was the hardest thing she'd ever done. Her three other children would be opening gifts on Christmas morning, and the oldest would have nothing. The mother felt she had to honour her daughter's request; instead of gifts, she filled the stocking with cards covered with written words of blessing and encouragement for her daughter.

• Christmas and the time just afterwards can be a very lonely time for many people even in our immediate neighbourhoods. For Christians, may God help us to reflect his heart for the lost, the abused, the poor, those in despair or darkness. Our children will often see into areas we have missed and let us not be afraid to follow through with their radical suggestions as to how we can make a real difference in someone's life. May God himself help us to see the need all around us and help us to offer a relevant alternative to the cynicism we meet all too often during the so-called 'festive' season. And may God help us to begin as we mean to go on, for there will be lonely, lost and needy people only a breath away from our comfortable lifestyles all the year round. We don't ever want our children to think that at Christmas we are generous towards those individuals and situations we turn a blind eye to for the rest of the year. What a challenge for us to follow Jesus throughout every season!

Meeting Jesus Means Change

How to help our children to learn to walk with Jesus every day, in every circumstance and situation. To demonstrate, by living it ourselves, that our relationship with Jesus is a golden thread running through the heart of every aspect of our existence, not something we 'do' on a Sunday or when we have a problem.

- Learn About Jesus – Make a chart with your children – it could simply be four sheets of A4 paper. Each piece of paper has headings as follows. Each time you find out something new, put that information on the chart under the relevant heading:

  The Bible: Read a selected passage of the Gospels each day and decide with your children what the passage is telling you about Jesus. You could also read many different passages in the Old and New Testaments to find descriptions of the nature and character of Jesus.

  Personal experience: What do your children know of Jesus by personal experience? Have they ever felt Jesus' touch? Have they experienced answered prayer? Have they heard his voice or felt his love? Have they experienced change in their lives because of Jesus? Let us pray without ceasing for our children, that from the earliest age, Jesus will touch their lives.

What parents say: What can you tell your children of Jesus from personal experience?

What other Christians say: Do you know people who have had encounters with Jesus, which it would be good for your children to hear about? Relay those stories to the children, via the specific individuals if possible. For example, there is a wonderful newsletter, which can be subscribed to by Internet. It is called *Friday Fax* and comes weekly. It is full of inspiring and encouraging true stories of what God is doing around the world in and through ordinary people.

- Pray with your children and ask Jesus to help you to know him better. Ask Jesus to touch your life and your children's lives. Sing songs of worship together. Do it while in the car driving somewhere or while walking at the seaside or while on a picnic.

- During an art time with your children, have everyone write a poem or a song or paint or draw a picture to express something you have learned about Jesus or something you have experienced. Treasure these creative expressions, share them with others where appropriate and place them in visible places around your home. Allow your home to become a unique and creative expression of the presence of Jesus. Your children will grow up in an environment where walking with the Lord is not an added extra, but rather an integral and natural part of their everyday life experience. According to Proverbs 22:6, we can trust God that our children will take these experiences with them into adulthood.

Example:

We know a family who believe they are called to the harvest: to play some part in reaching the world with the gospel. One of the family members has an evangelist's

MEETING JESUS MEANS CHANGE

heart, that is, he loves speaking to people about Jesus in the context of their own jobs or life experiences. Their home is littered with images and examples, there are living fish and wooden models of fish everywhere. Instead of indoor plants and flowers, there are bouquets of wheat sheaves. Their children have European and world maps on their walls and trinkets on their shelves from nations they are praying for. For a time, one of the children used a European flag to cover himself with as he slept at night. It was the flag of a particular nation he had a heart for, and had been praying for. Even the art displayed in the home demonstrated the family's heart for the gospel.

• Practise finding and noticing things in creation or in your surroundings which remind you of some facet of the nature of Jesus. Never tire of talking about them with your children.

Here are some simple examples:

– A hen gathering her chicks under her wing (Jesus' love is protective – Matthew 23:37);

– A foundation stone of a building (Jesus as the foundation of our salvation – 1 Peter 2:6);

– A book – note the author (Jesus as the author and perfecter of our faith – Hebrews 12:2);

– The night sky – talk about the morning star (Jesus as the bright Morning Star – Revelation 22:16);

– A wedding (Jesus' love for the church, like a bridegroom's love for his bride – Revelation 19:7; Ephesians 5:25-33).

• Cry out to God with your children, cry out to God for your children, pray the Scriptures, as in the following examples:

- Philippians 3:10 – 'I want to know Christ and the power of his resurrection, and the fellowship of sharing in his sufferings . . .'
- Revelation 22:20 – 'Come, Lord Jesus'
- Psalm 61:2 – 'From the ends of the earth I call to you, I call as my heart grows faith, lead me to the rock that is higher than I'
- Lamentations 2:11 – 'My eyes fail from weeping, I am in torment within, my heart is poured out on the ground because my people are destroyed, *because children and infants faint in the streets of the city.*'

Refiner's Fire

Helping our children to allow the Lord to mould and shape their lives on a daily basis. Walking in humility as a family. Learning to yield to or obey parents is good practice in learning to yield to God and to obey him. Helping our children to learn to take correction. Dealing with our own hypocrisies.

- It is important for parents to understand the distinction between character and anointing in their children. In terms of anointing, our children are our brothers and sisters in the Lord. We treat them as we would any other Christian; we can receive prayer, ministry, at times correction, and wisdom from them in the same way as we would from an adult brother or sister in the Lord. In terms of character, however, the parent–child functions come into play. Discipline is the responsibility of the parent and obedience is to be practised by the child. It is prudent to note that Timothy speaks much more of character than anointing. This is because character takes time and effort and perseverance and prayer to develop. Ungodly or underdeveloped character can destroy anointing, so the importance of the parent–child function with relation to character development cannot be overemphasised.

- In terms of the refining process in children's lives, parents should be extremely slow to habitually pick fault in their children. It is far better to practise regularly yielding to Jesus as a family. This does not always need to be through a time of prayer and can happen in practical ways. For instance, your child's lack of organisation may be affecting not only his or her bedroom but also the schoolwork. Why not use a chart to help your child develop a sense of responsibility for keeping a clean room? Why not use rewards to help children develop good housekeeping habits, which will be of great benefit throughout life? Why not *help* your child to clean his or her room, showing how it's done?

- God often deals with one or two particular issues in our lives at a given time, even though there may be many areas that need dealing with. It is far better to focus on one area of character development, where we can encourage our children each step of the way. With God's help, parents can recognise which area is being highlighted in their children's lives. Then they can help and encourage their children to respond to God in that specific area. There can be a temptation to highlight all the areas our children are at fault in ('. . . And you never tidy your room, you always leave your homework unfinished, and you are being rude again, how many times do I have to remind you to share your things . . .'). We can unwittingly heap a sense of overwhelming failure on our children, when we mean to shower them with a sense of approval and success. Let us allow God to have his way in our children's lives and let's participate in what he is doing.

- Pray in faith for your children. Pray into being the words that have been spoken over each one. Pray without ceasing for a soft heart and for your children to have a desire to yield to God. Pray for God's will every step of the way in your children's lives, pray for holiness in your family, in your home and in your relationships. Pray for God's provision for you as parents every step of the way. Pray for wisdom and help as you bring up your children. Pray as you do the housework, as you drive or as you go for a walk. Pray as you ride the bus or train. I used to be so upset if I awoke in the night, and was unable to get back to sleep. Now I am thrilled, and use that time to pray.

- Believe God is for you. Believe God's grace can cover any of your failures. Actively practise receiving God's grace every time you fail. Believe the best for you and your children. Dare to believe you do *not* have to repeat the mistakes that damaged you in your own upbringing. Really rely on God. Live by faith and trust him to help you. Believe his word: 'My grace is sufficient for you (that means – it's enough!); my strength is made perfect in weakness.' In other words, your weakness and failure as a parent qualifies you for God's grace. The greater your weakness, the greater his strength and the more you'll qualify for his strength to be at work in you, the greater his grace.

Example:

When our eldest son was younger, I felt very conscious about the mistakes I made with him during the day. I had never been a parent before and sometimes didn't discipline him appropriately, or didn't spend enough time with him, or was impatient or just made practical mistakes. The guilt I often felt at not being a good enough parent drove me to my knees. There I learned that God's grace is sufficient for any situation. A precious friend told me an incredible truth, which changed our lives. I could simply receive God's grace to cover my mistakes, and to redeem them in our son's life. This was amazing to me. Grace gave me freedom to learn from my mistakes and grace covered our son. We enjoyed every minute of his growing up and we see fruit in his life that can only have grown because of the goodness and grace of God.

• We often ask God for anointing in our function in the church meeting we go to, for example, that I can do the children's ministry well, or counsel people, or share the gospel or be a good intercessor, or a good 'Welcome Team' member. What about asking the Lord for sufficient anointing for raising our children? How often have we asked for anointing to share Jesus with them? What about asking God for anointing and grace to pray for our children and to parent them in a way that pleases him? The Bible promises that if we ask our Father for bread, he will not give us a stone (Matthew 7:9). Perhaps this seems obvious, but it was a revelation to us. We ask God's help in every other function we perform as Christians, yet we often forget the most important ministry, task or function we will ever undertake, which is to impart the kingdom to our children.

Responding to Jesus

Helping our children to recognise the Lord's touch in their lives, his presence, his voice, and to simply – respond. Never to ignore.

- Encourage and teach your children to respond simply and with their hearts to Jesus – that there can be a perpetual 'Yes Lord' response whenever they sense his presence. We don't have to be rigid – 'I asked Jesus into my heart last year – now I am a Christian and that's it! The Holy Spirit can convict us again and again to respond to Jesus. (Let's not be drawn into a theological debate about whether this is being 'saved' again and again and again!) We are simply talking about responding (the dictionary describes it as making an answer to) whenever Jesus comes near.

- Children need to be free to respond many times to Jesus, as their understanding and maturity grows. For example, our son first asked Jesus into his life at age 2½, but that didn't stop him from saying at age 12½, 'Jesus, I still want to follow you – today I am saying that I want you in my life forever – I am sorry for the wrong I've done and I want to follow you.' He couldn't remember what had happened ten years earlier, but he was now experiencing life situations that caused him to feel he had to make a conscious decision. God was definitely in his life as a result of his early prayer. He made many responses between the ages of 2 and 12 as the Holy Spirit moved him. Each response was precious. Each response was real. Each time the presence of Jesus as a result of his prayers was evident. Each time he experienced something more of the presence of Jesus and learned to know him a little more. Each time he took another step on his individual journey of faith.

- One of the best ways children can learn to respond to Jesus is by seeing their parents responding, most importantly and perhaps firstly, in the home, but also publicly. If you have responded to Jesus privately, then share it with your children. Where appropriate, tell your children what happened, how you knew Jesus was talking to you and what you did.

  Tell your children about the first time you responded to Jesus. Was it when you became a Christian? Share your most precious experiences of Jesus coming into your life with your children. Share many steps you took in your journey. It will touch them deeply and will also encourage them to share their experiences with you.

- We can teach our children that a response to Jesus can take many forms:

  - A quiet *personal response* from the heart, such as, 'Jesus, I love you and today I choose to serve and follow you.'

  - A *verbal response* spoken aloud while alone or by telling certain others, 'This is what Jesus said to me and I am responding to him.'

  - An *action (or repentance)* – 'I need to say sorry to my wife (husband/parents/child) for something I've said or done.'

- *Obedience* – 'I am going to give away a particular thing' or 'I am going to serve someone by baking a cake or visiting them or cutting their grass' or 'I am going to choose to forgive (a specific person).

- *Repentance* – 'I am going to make a change' in a particular area of life.

• It's good to teach our children to seek the prayers of someone we trust as we respond to Jesus. This will often happen if we respond in a public meeting, especially in the context of our local faith community gathering where we are in a safe, loving family environment. As parents we can model receiving prayer from others during a time of response. Let's encourage our children in the following ways:

- Encourage your children and pray that they will be able to see when their non-Christian friends make some response to Jesus, that your children can see their friends as God sees them.

- Encourage your children to then speak to their friends and encourage the responses those friends have made.

- Encourage your children to pray for their friends.

Example:

A young boy we know had a good friend throughout his school years. The boy literally led his friend to Jesus. When they were 8 or 9, he asked the friend, 'Do you want to become a Christian? Then just pray after me . . .' The boy actively discipled his friend through the years. He encouraged the friend to respond in integrity and righteousness through many different circumstances. When asked how this could happen, the little boy's parent said, 'My son told me what was happening at school, I discipled my child and he discipled his friend.'

- We can miss what God is doing and sometimes just don't see his hand in the lives of others or in different situations. So with your children, 'ask' to see God's work in the lives of school friends, for example, and 'ask' for the ability to help and encourage them.

- Help your children to see when their school friends are expressing godly virtues like compassion, honesty, acting with justice and so on, so that they can encourage these friends.

  For example: In secondary school, one of the boys in Jane's class had his backpack stolen by some boys who were bullying him. They threw the backpack around the playground and some cooking he had done in school burst inside the pack, ruining many of his books. A non-Christian friend called Rella was standing beside Jane and was laughing at the boy's plight. Jane encouraged Rella to see the situation from the injured boy's perspective. Rella became quickly compassionate and together the girls found a teacher, stopped the bullies and tried to act in whatever way they could to help both the teacher's investigations and the boy who had been mistreated.

- We can respond to Jesus in times of prayer, intercession, praise or worship when we sense the Holy Spirit drawing us. When this happens in the home, respond to Jesus, pray or praise and draw your children in on what is happening. Be ready for your children to be 'called' to prayer or worship or warfare and join in with all your heart.

  Example:

  We know a family where the parents often listen with their children to a cassette tape that has blessed or encouraged them or that is relevant to their family situation. The parents explain why they enjoyed the tape and why they wanted their children to hear it. Lively discussion often followed.

In our family we as parents read a wonderful book called *Reconnecting the Generations* by a lady called Daphne Kirk (Kevin Mayhew, 2002). We then read parts of the book to our children, explained why the book meant so much to us, and discussed the ideas together and in the light of Scripture.

- Responding to Jesus in practical ways is just as important as responding in spiritual ways. As a parent, one of the ways you may be responding for the next six months is to take your child out for breakfast every four weeks. To your child, a response may be to do the washing up without complaining. (Despite the temptation, it must be our child's own response and not ours: 'You have to respond to Jesus by doing the washing up.')

All Have Sinned –
Getting Right with God

Helping children understand the concept of sin and separation from God. Helping them along their own personal journey of getting right with God. Encouraging children to get hold of the great hope and good news we have in Jesus.

- Pray for your children that God will give them an understanding of salvation from a very young age. Use examples and stories from your own life and the life experiences of friends wherever possible.

Examples:

When I read *The Lion the Witch and the Wardrobe* for the first time, over 20 years ago, through what happened to Edmund I received an incredible revelation of what Jesus did for me. Even though I had known and pursued the Lord for many years before this event, it was only as I read C. S. Lewis' book that I 'saw' for the first time the incredible price Jesus paid for *me* personally. The sharing of my experience was helpful to our children, because it gave them a life example of the great benefits to each of us if we have a personal and heaven-inspired revelation of what Jesus did at the cross.

Through a church youth event, while a video of the crucifixion was played, one of the teenage boys had a personal revelation of salvation – of the great sacrifice Jesus had made for him. He was changed forever; he was profoundly impacted. His response was to worship Jesus in a way he had never done before. He wrote an amazing piece of poetry expressing the majesty and goodness of God. Now he 'knows' that Jesus died for him, and nobody can present an argument that will sway him. Now his 'belief' is grounded on personal experience.

- Explain salvation to your children in many ways; use word pictures; use object lessons. Do it over many years; share what you learn and share the things that touch your heart. Tell your children when suddenly you have a new revelation of salvation or a new understanding of some aspect of Jesus' sacrifice for us.

Example:

An interesting word picture of what Jesus did at the cross is as follows: We were in prison and nobody had the key to unlock the door to get us out into freedom. Jesus came and had the only key that would fit the lock. It was shaped like a cross. He opened the door, let us out, went in and served our punishment.

- Share with your children Scriptures on being born again, and on being saved such as:
  – John 3:16; Acts 2:21; Acts 4:12; Romans 10:9
- Pray for understanding, for yourself and for your children, of the grace of God as directly related to his gift of salvation:
  – Ephesians 2:5, 8; John 1:17; Acts 15:11; Romans 3:24; 5:2; 2 Corinthians 8:9, to name but a few of many wonderful verses.

- Share your experiences in your own journey of faith with your children. Your experiences will bless, challenge and inspire them to pursue Jesus for themselves.

Example:

A dad shared this example with his children: 'I was backslidden; that means I was not living as a Christian. I was not living as a friend of God. I was living in a way that made me far away from God. One day I was standing in a town square listening to some people talk about the Christian gospel. Somebody came up behind me and said, "Do you know that Jesus loves you?" I did know and his words were like a knife in my heart. From that day I began to come back to the Lord. I turned back to Jesus during the singing of a song called "Take Me Back" by Andre Crouch. The words were all about asking the Lord to take *me* back and help *me* to remember the day I first received his love and the day I first believed. Then one day soon afterwards I got baptised and was amazed to realise that the very same song, "Take me back", was playing during my baptism. Nobody knew that song was special to me and it was on a tape of many songs; it just happened to be that one which was playing during my baptism. I knew God was with me and that he had made this happen; a sign on earth to demonstrate heaven's gladness at my decision.'

- Keep short accounts with God, with your spouse and with your children; be quick to repent and quick to confess when you get it wrong. If this is your way of life, your children will copy you.

- Practise actively receiving God's forgiveness, then let go of your guilt and lay it down, and be encouraged by the book of Romans, 4:7-8; 5:1-2; 8:38. Again, your children will 'do as you do'.

- Help your children to understand the difference between conviction and condemnation. Conviction can be a sweet experience: I love who I discipline. When we confess our sins God truly is faithful and just and forgives us our sins and does in reality cleanse us from all unrighteousness (1 John 1:9). We experience the wonderful approval of God our Father in spite of our mistakes. Once we turn from our sin conviction is very releasing: we are set free.

  On the other hand, condemnation is heavy and bitter, and produces a nagging feeling of guilt, which will not let up. Condemnation is like having a heavy chain around our necks, dragging us down; it is almost like a death sentence. The Bible clearly states that there is no condemnation for those who are in Jesus (Romans 8:1). This doesn't mean a little condemnation, or a little bit of self-imposed penance on our part; we do not have to suffer to pay for our sins. Condemnation for the Christian should be non-existent! What a wonderful revelation for us – to be able to live in the constant love and approval of God our Father, even when he is disciplining us.

- Pray for your children, that God would give them a heart that is soft and open to him.

Sowing and Reaping

Teaching our children, through everyday life experiences, to sow good seed in their own lives and the lives of others. Helping them to find forgiveness, God's grace and his goodness in times when they are living in the consequences of unhelpful or even bad seed sown in times past. Helping our children to understand the importance of our individual confession, our attitudes and the choices we make.

- In the home, where God calls us to correct and disciple our children, it is so important to do so without personal condemnation. It is equally important for ourselves and for our children to be able to receive the grace of God when we fail. When we, as parents, are totally at the end of our own reserves, exasperated with negative behaviour or outright defiance on the part of our children, it is then we need the power of God. When anger rises up in our own hearts, we need the Holy Spirit more than ever to help us to display self-control – well before we stand against our children's unacceptable behaviour. We can bring discipline or correction as a consequence of that behaviour, while at the same time clearly affirming our children.

- Plant a small patch of ground as a family. Each person can choose seeds or plants to put in it. Have the children water and weed the patch with you. You can use a tub if there is no available ground space or if you do not have a garden. Remind your children that as the Holy Spirit waters our lives, the seeds, which have been planted there, will also grow. Pray together that God will help you all to sow good seed in your own and in one another's lives.

Examples:

Many parents and teachers already plant seeds with their children. It is an activity that is often already scheduled in and is a part of their lives and their education. What could be simpler than to bring the Lord into this activity? Why not say something like, 'When we're planting these seeds, it's just like the seeds we plant in other people's lives by the things we say or how we treat them. We know that marigolds are going to grow from these seeds. Did you know that the "seeds" we plant in other people's lives also grow up into something? Did you know that we can actually plant sadness or hurt, or even a wrong understanding into people's lives, just by what we say to them and how we treat them? Why don't we ask Jesus to help us to always plant good things in the lives of others?'

I'll never forget when we had a guest speaker come to our house to speak with a group of teenage boys we were meeting with. He brought a tube of strong toothpaste and a saucer. He told us that we had to be so careful with our words. 'Once you say something,' he said, squeezing the tube, 'it's out and you can't take it back, just like you can't get the toothpaste back into this tube.' It was a simple, though extremely powerful, lesson (accompanied by a strong smell of mint) that those children will not soon forget.

- Realise that your own words sow seeds in your children's lives. Are we sowing disapproval – are we sowing negative words (*'You're so clumsy'* or *'Stop being so stupid'*) – are we using sarcasm or cynicism against our children? Negative words can pierce a child's self-esteem in an instant and bring insecurity and rejection. How much do we say, 'I love you' to our children? Do we just say it when they have 'done' something well or performed well? Do we ever say it when they have failed miserably at something? How often do we say, 'I love you' for no obvious reason, and not as a result of some great performance? Ask God to give you a greater ability to be an affirmer in your home. Ask for eyes to see beyond the obvious so that you can encourage your children for who they are and not for what they do.

- If you have failed to speak to your children in a way that pleases God, go quickly for mercy and grace to cover your mistakes. Repent as often as it takes, while sincerely asking and believing that God's grace will bring healing to your children. Remember that repentance is a sincere turning around and rely on God's help to make your own adjustments. Rely on the Holy Spirit to help you to verbally bless and encourage your children. Believe that God's grace is bigger than your failures; receive that grace and learn to humbly walk in it. Believe that his grace is sufficient to heal any hurt which your words or actions may have caused your child.

- Teach your children that they can sow seeds in each other's lives and pray with them that God will literally anoint their tongues to speak encouragement, blessing, healing words, affirmation to their brothers and sisters and friends. Extend your own grace when your children fail. Learn not to have unrealistic expectations or to set impossible standards that set them up for failure.

- Go a step further with your children by helping them learn to see God's heart for others and then to speak prophetically into others' lives. In doing this they can sow seeds of destiny and calling. Our prophetic words can help to birth seeds of faith, healing, hope and vision into the lives of others. Help your children to check out what they feel God has given them for someone else, by telling you or by telling their home group or cell group leader. Also help them learn to give what they have received in an appropriate way.

- Spend time with your children, chatting through situations they have encountered and attitudes they may have. Discuss with your children in advance what choices can be made as to how to act in certain situations, which will cause good seeds to grow in their lives and the lives of others. For example, if brothers and sisters are at odds, chat with each one and discuss how they could relate in a more godly way or how they could break out of the negative circle of each one always trying to have the last word.

- Discuss what the fruit may be of attitudes your children are displaying. Don't just do it when they have done wrong. Do it as encouragement when you see godly attitudes or behaviour (such as unselfishness or kindness, for example, '*Did you know that your kind words to Jo today are going to be like soothing cream on a wound? Your words will bring a touch of Jesus' kindness to Jo's life*'). Have many more times of this type of discussion for positive attitudes than negative ones.

- Encourage your children to take the initiative in a situation rather than passively accepting the bad behaviour of others in school. *'It wasn't my fault – they were all calling Sam names – I just stood there – I didn't call him names.'* In a situation like this, encourage your children: first of all, bless them if they simply stood there – bless your children for not following the crowd. Then talk over some of the following ideas to help your children through similar future situations they may face:

  – 'What might Jesus have said in this situation?'
  – 'What could you have said that would have stopped the name calling, or helped the victim, or brought God's word into the mix?'

- Give your children ideas of different and new ways of relating to classmates and behaving, which express God's kingdom, as an alternative to just 'being a passive bystander or following the crowd'. Also, encourage your child's own ideas as to how to express God's kingdom in a situation.

Forgiveness

We can best model God's forgiveness towards our children if we are walking in it ourselves. How we, as parents and guardians, can lead in repentance by our own attitudes and behaviour, which have a far greater effect on the children in our care than our words do. How we can model God's own heart for our children, by modelling unconditional, unmerited forgiveness towards them.

An Encouragement for Parents

- We don't have to be perfect! Children need to know that their parents sin as well, that we make mistakes too. Let's not hide our mistakes, but lead the way in modelling true repentance (not piety) and forgiveness.

- A family where there is no conflict, including conflict between spouses, is probably non-existent. We need to have realistic expectations of our children and ourselves. We do not need to be afraid of conflict; on the contrary, it's healthy for our children to see a godly resolution of that conflict. It is healthy for them to see us resolve problems and walk through disagreements.

- Get into the habit of confessing sin to one another. Parents can not only lead the way by doing it and coming to their

111

children for forgiveness when they've 'messed up', but can also encourage their children to do the same.

- How important it is to treat one another, everyone in our family, with honour. Sometimes we need to practise speaking to one another as if they were strangers or visitors. How many of us need to learn to treat our own spouse or our own children with at least as much honour and respect as we would treat a visitor?

- In a family, where not much can be hidden and where everyone's weak points are intimately known, there can be a great temptation to either bring up past failures or to make sweeping statements, which are not strictly true:

  - *'You always have to have the last word'* or *'You always start the fight.'*
  - *'You never speak kindly to me.'*
  - *'The last three times this happened you told a lie; I think you are lying now.'*

As parents, we can be just as guilty of this negative accusation as our children; let's yield to the Holy Spirit and learn not only to temper our strong words, but also to resist the temptation to use our knowledge of a spouse's or child's past failures against them now.

- Have family discussion times, where everyone has an equal voice, to deal with current issues. For example, 'We are in the habit of speaking unkindly to each other.' Find out everyone's perspective on the problem and through discussion and prayer decide together, 'How are we going to deal with this problem? How can we co-operate with God and learn to live in a different way?' At times, where everyone in the family is part of a problem, repent together by confessing to God and to each other. Receive God's forgiveness together. Find practical ways to learn to live differently. Learn to encourage one another.

- Break in yourself the habit of living under guilt or in condemnation and do not condemn your children for their mistakes. God's forgiveness means that we have no need to ever live this way and our children need to be free of it. Stress with your children the joy of being made clean; teach about God's love and his father heart. Teach your children scriptures about God's forgiveness and his mercy. Read the story of the prodigal son together (Luke 15).

- Help your children to practise keeping short accounts before God. Teach them to recognise the conviction of the Holy Spirit and how to deal with sin immediately. When you pray with your children, make time for waiting on God and being open to the Holy Spirit's conviction of sin. Every day can be a new day; we never have to carry yesterday's failings around with us today. Help your children to live in this truth.

- Ask for God's help in giving unconditional love and approval to your children right alongside their confession of sin and your possible discipline as a result of that sin. Our children need to know that they are acceptable to us, no matter how greatly they fail. That is God's heart for us. There is no doubt that our children or youth may shock us by their wrongs; in these cases we need to guard ourselves lest we react against the child because of the embarrassment or trouble they may have caused us.

- Use your own prophetic insight and encourage your children to use theirs to respond to God in real, creative ways. For example, a family we know came to a place where they felt they were not honouring each other much any more. It was a bit of the 'familiarity breeds contempt' syndrome, where family members began to take each other for granted, and shortness and sharpness of tone were becoming commonplace. The parents increasingly became convicted by the words in Hebrews 6:8 and wanted God to burn up the thorns and thistles in all their lives. With the children, they collected small, dead twigs, bits of dried leaf, thorns and thistles and made a small fire on the back garden patio. The twigs, etc., symbolised the sin in their lives, the way they were treating each other. They prayed that God would come and burn up the sin in their lives. The fire symbolised the fire of God to clean them inside. The family prayed and yielded to God together for his touch in their lives. Each child prayed aloud, from their heart, as did the parents. Together they thanked God for his forgiveness and for his ongoing help in their relationships together. They also looked at practical ways to treat each other with honour. The prophetic act they engaged in was not a solution, nor was it a magic end to their troubles. It was the first step; there would be steps forward and steps backward, but it was a turning to a new way of living, and every member of that family realised that they could only walk consistently forward with God's help on a daily basis.

Revival

To grow in your children a desire and a hunger to see real revival in their own lives; in other words a deeper passion for Jesus and an explosion of growth in their relationship with him. Alongside this, how to grow in your children a sensitivity to the heart of God for the lost in your neighbourhood, your town, your nation and other nations. How to help your children understand the nature of true revival by exposing them to today's revival stories from around the world.

- Find out about revival stories from books, the Internet and connections your church may have with other churches. Share these stories with your children on a regular basis and pray together for the people and situations you read about.

  Examples:

  Subscribe to revival Newsletters by Internet, such as *Friday Fax, Revival Chinese Ministries International* and *Joel News.* Get newsletters from ministries such as Toybox Charity working into Guatemala, Iris Ministries in Mozambique and Metro Ministries International in New York City. Meet with and hear from Christian missionaries you know, or who are known and supported by your church.

- Pray and ask God to help you as a family to find a way to make a difference or to participate in some of the revival situations you have heard about. It may be that God speaks to your children in answer to your own prayers. Be willing and ready to respond.

  Example:

  A family we know became interested in helping children with disabilities partly due to the children's relationship with the founder of a disability ministry. This led to them buying a wheelchair for a child in Africa. The family now have a photograph of a special person sitting in the wheelchair they paid for.

- Help your children continue with a 'Milestones in My Life' book, where they keep a written and pictorial record of important events in their walk with God. Take seriously their dreams, visions, prayers and the words and pictures they receive from God. Keep your own record of your child's walk with God. From time to time, go over with your child the things you've recorded. Go through the 'Milestones' book together; pray over those things and thank God for his word. Practise helping your child to actively receive the words that have been spoken over him or her.

- Believe that God can and wants to do great things beyond what you have imagined, beyond your prayers, beyond your dreams – in and through your children. Pray, pray, pray for a release of his Spirit in their lives and call in his future for your children.

- Ask God to pour out a hunger for revival and all that entails, on you and in *your* home. When he does, *you will* have a major effect on your children.

- Help your children to respond appropriately to what God has given them, to what they have heard from God the Holy Spirit. You may find your children have encounters with God which are new to you, which are even beyond your understanding. For example, what if your child sees an angel? What do you do? What if your child has an intense time of intercession and begins to pray in a way that is completely new to you?

Example:

In our family we have encountered each of these situations and following are some of the things we have learned.

One of the first things we, as parents, can do is to pray and ask God for wisdom and understanding to guide and encourage our children. We can also ask God in faith to teach us as he is teaching our children. What does the Scripture say about what our children are experiencing? It may be necessary for *us* to learn about intercession, for example, so that we can help our children. Look for Christian books that have a wise and helpful perspective on the specific situation you are encountering. For example, Dutch Sheets has written very helpful books about intercession. It's also helpful and practical to simply ask someone we respect. If they can't help they may be able to point to someone who can. Additionally you may know someone who has experience in the area you need to learn about.

- What if God the Holy Spirit tells your child he/she is to help a lonely person in the neighbourhood or what if your child expresses a desire to pray for a particular nation or people group? This will be an amazing opportunity for you to help your child to respond to God; it may also mean some of your time and commitment to stand with your child and even to follow the Holy Spirit's instructions with them.

- It is important in any of these situations, even if you feel you know how your children should respond to their encounter with God, to share the whole experience with one or two people who:
  - understand your situation,
  - know you well,
  - carry something of God's heart for children,
  - have some experience dealing with children and the supernatural.

Sharing your experiences with others means that your teaching and discipling of your children can be done within the safety and covering of godly relationships.

- It is important to cover your children and important to resist the urge to spread their story everywhere: *My child was profoundly touched by God – he/she had a vision!* etc. Especially after an encounter with God, our children are very vulnerable and very sensitive to spiritual backlash, lack of adult understanding of their experience, adult cynicism and unbelief ('kids can't hear from God'), wrong public exposure or inappropriate adult responses to them. Any of these reactions can cause confusion in our children or can undermine what God has done. If we share our child's experience with one or two trusted people with the above qualifications, we can avoid the dangers.

Example:

We know a 7-year-old girl who has an amazing gift in praying for other people. She seems to pray right to the point, and seems to hear God's heart. Her parents were exhibiting magazine materials at a large Christian conference.

The little girl put out a 'prayer chair' at her parent's exhibition stand and offered to pray for everyone who visited. Her mother simply prayed and asked the Holy Spirit to guide her daughter's prayers and to tell her what to pray for people. Many people were deeply touched by the little girl's prayers, some wept at the way her prayers spoke exactly into their circumstances or situations. The parents resisted the urge to publicise their daughter's gift. Instead they chose to quietly nurture it, to yield their daughter and her gifts to the Lord, and to humbly seek his help. In order to encourage their daughter they realised they may not personally be well enough equipped so they decided to get in touch with a lady they knew who had mentored many young children in powerful prayer. (This story has been shared with the parents' permission.)

We need to be very careful before we put spiritually gifted children onto a platform and publicly expose them, particularly when the Lord has not asked us to. It is a good thing to sincerely want others in the body of Christ to understand the amazing things children can accomplish when anointed by God. There will be appropriate ways of telling amazing stories without subjecting individual children to the dangers that come with public exposure.

Salt and Light

How to help our children to experience God's own heart for the lost; for those people everywhere who don't yet know Jesus. How to help our children to respond to God and to participate in issues of poverty and social justice from an early age.

- Pray for yourself and your children and be open to receiving a heart for the lost. It is something only God can give and is often a result of a renewed passion for Jesus or simply of getting closer to God's own heart, which burns with compassion for the lost (John 3:16).

- Then, with your children, connect with Jesus! Pray 'Jesus help us, Jesus lead us, Jesus guide us. What are you asking *us* to do – to give – to be part of – to spend our time and money on? Following are some examples of possible responses we can make.

- Get connected with an organisation such as VIVA Network, which exists specifically for the lost, the poor, the underprivileged, the marginalised. If you have a computer, you can look up their website. Connect with organisations such as Esther Network, which aims to mobilise a million children to pray for their generation. Find out about organisations such as Care for the Family.

- Get involved in the suffering of the nations, not only by being informed but also practically (you could sponsor a child through Compassion International, for instance):

  - Give as a family: give pocket money, time, resources, energy, prayer.

  - Get involved with local issues of injustice, such as in the local school or borough, or neighbourhood. Get involved in a way that would reflect the heart of Jesus and would be appropriate for your children to participate in, in some way.

  - Get involved with your neighbours. Look for and pray for opportunities to serve and bless them as a family. Prayer walk around your street again and again. Welcome the presence of Jesus. Get excited and exercise faith; prepare the way for the coming King, just as John the Baptist did (Luke 3:4-6).

  - Find out about Fair Trade organisations and choose to buy products that are produced in a way that upholds the rights of the local workers in the country of origin.

  - 10 per cent of the world's population live on 70 per cent of the world's resources. What is Jesus asking of your family as a kingdom response and a kingdom lifestyle?

- It is important to model and teach your children not to be driven by the needs around them, which will be many. We can become swallowed up by the injustice, pain and suffering around us, completely spend ourselves on behalf of the lost and become lost ourselves in the process. Then we will be of little benefit to Jesus, our family or the lost. Rather, teach your children to respond to Jesus and to live in the power of such

Scriptures as Isaiah 40:28-31; Psalm 37:5-6; Psalm 127:1 and Isaiah 61:1-4. Teach your children to seek – 'what is Jesus asking of me today?' or 'what would Jesus do in this situation?'

- Pray for the lost with your children (the lost: those people who do not know Jesus or who have never heard the Christian gospel). Learn about different nations and pray for them. Pray for different people groups: the homeless, children of all ages, the poor, those in prison, the sick, people who are mentally or physically disabled. Find creative ways to get practically involved. Find creative ways to pray. Get a globe, for example, and pray over it with your children. Put your arms around the globe and pray Jesus' love to be manifested or made visible in the nations. Encourage your children to hear from God. Write the names of specific children or nations on till rolls (you can put literally hundreds of names on a till roll and when rolled up, it is still very small and lightweight), roll them up and carry them around in your pocket.

- Use maps of the world in your home. Make your home a prophetic symbol of what God has spoken to you about. For example, a friend we know who is very practically involved in issues of justice in a number of European countries has painted words such as freedom on large pieces of coloured cloth and hung them up in her home. She and her husband have tastefully hung the flag of a country they are involved in. Another family has decorated their living area with pictures and models of fish and sheaves of wheat because of the heart God has given them for the lost and the vision he has given them for a great harvest of people from every nation. Another friend filled every large jar and pot she could find with water and put the pots in the hall just inside the front entrance of their home. They wanted to symbolise the water and the rain of God falling into their home. Another family brought some small pieces of raw salt into their home as encouragement to each of them to be like salt. Jesus said, 'You are the salt of the earth.'

- Talk with your children about the Great Commission in Matthew 28. Pray about it together and ask God to help you to respond to Jesus' challenge to 'go and make disciples.' Talk with your children about what the Scripture means. Relate it to your everyday life wherever possible.

- Find published resources such as the book *Window on the World* by Daphne Spraggett with Jill Johnstone (published by Angus Hudson Ltd) and use them with your children. This revised version is colourful and well written and applicable for both children and teens.

The Holy Spirit

How to introduce young children to the person of the Holy Spirit and how to help them relate to the Holy Spirit in everyday life. Helping your children experience the presence and power of the Holy Spirit in their day-to-day lives.

- Practise literally welcoming the Holy Spirit with open arms, into your home, by simply saying, 'Welcome Holy Spirit.' Welcome God the Holy Spirit into your bedrooms, your heart, your relationships, your games – in short, into every area of your lives. Do it verbally, out loud, so your children can hear you and encourage them to do the same. Young children will naturally copy your words and actions. Initially it may be just copying, but because of the life of God poured out through the Holy Spirit, because of the Lord's own desire to touch these children, it will soon become a personal experience for them. Always encourage your children to talk about how they feel, so that you can assure them, encourage them, teach them and lead them on.

Example:

A lady we know makes a practice of simply sitting in her room, saying, 'Come, Holy Spirit.' She sits in his presence for a few hours each week. She says that is where she finds refreshing, rest and healing.

Why not lie on the carpet with your children, each in your own space? Put on a worship CD and simply 'rest' in the Lord's presence for five minutes, ten minutes or more.

- Receive from God a love for the Holy Spirit and let your children see that love by the way you model it. Pray that God will give them a love for the Holy Spirit as well.

- Grow in your own ability to recognise the Holy Spirit's presence, then acknowledge that presence and tell your children when you sense it, whenever you sense the Holy Spirit is near. Ask your children to tell you when they sense the Holy Spirit's presence. Talk about how they feel, what they see and hear and then respond together.

- Be willing to hear from God the Holy Spirit through your children. Tell your children when he gives you something for them. Encourage your children when you notice them speaking in a way that is inspired by God.

  Example:

  One little girl we know 'saw' a mighty wave as if from an ocean, crashing over the school gates and into the schoolyard. She believed it was a wave of revival that God was going to bring into the schoolyard. We took her very seriously. We thanked God, we prayed to welcome the Holy Spirit into that school and we acknowledged him whenever we saw evidence of his presence in a child's life or a situation.

- Cultivate in yourself and in your child, sensitivity to the Holy Spirit and a desire to learn to live in the presence of God. We are not speaking about over-spirituality or about living out of touch with the world – on the contrary!

Living in the presence of Jesus will put us much more in touch with the world. The minute our children step out of our doors to go to school or other activities, we are no longer always there to shield and protect them, but God the Holy Spirit can be. With all the danger, despair and doubt which bombards our children on a daily basis, there is no better covering for them than his presence.

Example:

We know of a young boy, aged 8, who prayed the following prayer. His mum carefully recorded as much as she could during the ten minutes the boy was praying. She gave us permission to share this prayer, to encourage other parents. Our children are capable of so much more than we give them credit for. Our children are able to pray out of inspiration from the Holy Spirit and way beyond their years. 'He prayed that God would be real to him, not because of mum and dad but because of his choice, and continued as follows:

Lord, please give us back in blessing what we give.
Do not let anyone curse the ground we walk on.
Life is like a card game and Satan has run out of Jokers
    and Queens and 2s and God has given me all the cards.

'He prayed for the Lord to help him use his choice of cards carefully and use his mind carefully:

Lord, please give me things to do with preventing your
    plans getting wrecked.
Lord, please help me to be good.
Lord, please help my family and me to be in the book of
    life.
Please help me to be strong about what I say;
when the enemy reminds me about my past, I can remind

> him about his future: Greater is he that is in me, than
> he that is in the world' (1 John 4:4).

- Together with your child, find a short time near the beginning of each day to welcome the Holy Spirit into your home and into your life. Ask for him to fill you and yield to his purposes.

- Cultivate a love for the Holy Spirit yourself and ask him to help you to pass this on to your children. Your children are never too young. We asked the Holy Spirit to fill our three children when they were 4½, 3 and 1 year old. It was a wonderful time and the results were dramatic and sustained. Each of the children also began to pray in a wonderful new way. In speaking about being filled with the Holy Spirit, we are not speaking of a one-off experience, such as in the 'baptism of the Holy Spirit', but rather about a life-long journey.

- Ask your child/children to pray for you to be filled with the Holy Spirit.

- When your children talk about their pressures, problems or anxieties at school, bring in the Holy Spirit. Remind your children that he is the Comforter (John 14:16, American Standard Version). Also remind them of his power to help them in difficulties. God the Holy Spirit doesn't always help us to escape from a difficult situation but to cope and grow and have his presence *through* it. Pray through situations with your children. Note those situations which seem to change for the better and thank God together for the presence of his Spirit – in other words, acknowledge the Holy Spirit when a situation changes and do not put it down to coincidence.

- A challenge to parents that we, as children's group leaders, have had to face. Do I believe Acts 1:8? Do I believe that

I will receive power to proclaim Jesus when the Holy Spirit comes upon me? This is what we are teaching our children to believe. Have I personally experienced the filling and the power of the Holy Spirit?

- Following is a book for recommended reading, not because of its author's theology or way of conducting a large meeting. It is guaranteed that many of us may disagree with both of the above. The book, *Good Morning Holy Spirit* by Benny Hinn (Thomas Nelson, 1990), is recommended purely because of the author's great love for and devotion to Jesus by hearing, being in the presence of and obeying the Holy Spirit. Laying aside our personal perspectives to do with American TV evangelists, that theme alone makes wonderful and challenging reading.

Fruits of the Spirit

How to cultivate the fruit of the Holy Spirit (love, joy, peace, patience, kindness, gentleness, faithfulness, self-control, Galatians 5:22) in the lives of our children.

- It is impossible to hide our fruit or lack of it at home. Let's trust God to give us all we need not only to parent our children in a way that is pleasing to him, but also trust in God's ability to bring about his fruit in our own lives.

  If we allow our children to see our failings, they will feel they too are allowed freedom to fail. Let's make sure they see us responding to God in the *midst* of a time of failure. Don't expect your children to be perfect but rather encourage them when you see some fruit of the Spirit in their lives, however small it is. No matter how many times they fail, make sure your children come out of every failure feeling forgiven, clean and accepted. Persevere in confident prayer with your children for growth of fruit of the Spirit. The Bible says we should always pray and not give up.

- Someone has said that success is the ability to get through failure. God's agenda in our lives is not usually the same as our own. He works in areas of our character at his convenience and in his timing, which is often different to our own. We wonder if we are ever going to be victorious over a certain character trait that needs changing; we sometimes feel like giving up. So encourage your children in patience and perseverance, especially when they have behaved in the same old way yet again. We need to remember that our lives are like a journey through which God *will* grow the fruit of the Spirit as we yield to him. This is far from passivity; our active response is to yield and to be willing to change our attitudes and behaviour in co-operation with God the Holy Spirit whenever we feel his touch on those areas he is dealing with.

- A challenge to parents: It is very easy to display the fruit of the Spirit in a public Christian meeting, but it is at home, behind our closed doors, that what is in our hearts is truly exposed. We never want to teach our children it is OK to behave one way at 'church' and another at home. This is religion, which Jesus hated. We are called to be followers of Jesus and to disciple our children in a way that will encourage them to be the same.

- Don't push your children too hard to 'be good' in their own strength. According to the Bible, it is God who works in us to will and to act according to his good purpose (Philippians 2:13) and he is able to complete the good work he began in each of us (Philippians 1:6). Put these verses up in your home and refer to them often.

Example:

We have done the following exercise with our children. Get a large backpack and put it on your child's back. Gradually fill the backpack with very heavy books while you say, 'Don't lie, don't swear, don't succumb to temptations of drugs.' When the backpack is full, begin to fill their arms with heavy books while you continue by saying, 'Don't be a bully, don't be proud, don't follow the crowd, be a leader, pray, share Jesus.' How can our children succeed in carrying this heavy weight of our expectations for their behaviour if they don't even know how to live by faith in Jesus? How can they succeed if they are doing it all in their own strength? Jesus said, 'My yoke is easy.' We burden our children with such a weight of expectations about how they should live.

Then we have simply said to our children, 'Can you walk easily while you are carrying all this weight?' After their obvious response and as we have taken the books out of their arms and out of the backpack, we have said, 'We want to lift all these expectations, all these rules, off of you. All we ask of you is that you learn to know Jesus. This is our one request. It is only in his strength that you can live a holy life. It is only if you are full of Jesus that you can live in a way that pleases him. It is only out of his strength and his holiness in you!'

- Encourage your children by example to be primarily concerned with knowing Jesus, loving Jesus and being filled with his Spirit. At the end of the day, we don't change ourselves. We follow Jesus. Jesus changes us!

- Tell your children when you see the fruit of the Holy Spirit in their lives. Tell them when you see love, joy, peace, patience, kindness, gentleness, faithfulness, and self-control operating in them.

Giants in our Lives

Walking with our children through their times of fear, anxiety, self-doubt and insecurity. Taking their hands and helping them to cultivate a strong trust in God and in his ability to put to death those things which bind us and which seem so insurmountable. Even children have giants: situations, experiences, character traits, which cause them pain, fear and a feeling of defeat – and hinder them from being all God made them to be. Following are practical ways to help your children walk as David walked, when he said to Goliath: 'You come against me with sword and spear and javelin, but I come against you in the name of the Lord Almighty . . .' (1 Samuel 17:45).

- Following are many Scriptures that are positive responses to many so-called giants people face in everyday life, giants such as fear, guilt and anger. Here is an encouragement for parents: please read these Bible verses regularly to your children. It may be good to spend a week at a time reading all the verses to do with freedom from fear, for example. We can only imagine the wonderful benefit to our children, not only spiritually but also emotionally and physically, if they are raised on a regular diet of God's word. We hope these

Scriptures are also an encouragement to parents to actively use God's word in dealing with giants in their own lives.

Fear: Isaiah 41:10; Hebrews 13:5b-6; Psalm 27:1; Psalm 23:4; 1 John 4:18; Psalm 34:4; Romans 8:15-16

Guilt: Romans 3:23-24; Romans 8:1; Isaiah 53:66

Worry: Matthew 10:29-31; 1 Peter 5:7; Philippians 4:6-7; Matthew 6:33-34; Psalm 42:5

Insecurity (not feeling safe): Psalm 61:2-3; Deuteronomy 33:27; Isaiah 49:15-16; Matthew 10:29-31; Psalm 4:8; Psalm 121

Anger: Philippians 4:7; Ephesians 4:22-24; Romans 8:38; Galatians 5:16

Financial Worry: Philippians 4:19; Luke 12:15; 1 Timothy 6:17; Proverbs 3:5-6; Luke 12:33

Times of Trouble: Psalm 46:1-2; Romans 8:28

- Make a note of what other 'giants' exist in your own life and the lives of your children. Find Scriptures to counteract these giants and use those Bible verses in the same way.
- Pray with your children about the giants in your life (where appropriate) and in theirs. Let this be during the course of everyday life and on an ongoing basis. Invite your children to pray for you and be ready to receive God's insight into your situation through the mouths of your children. Receive ministry and prayer from your children with humility and as you would receive ministry from an adult.

Examples:

Fear of Spiders

Many children have a fear of spiders or creepy crawlies. It's easy to belittle their fears, e.g. 'Don't be so silly' we say, forgetting our own childish fears. It is far better to pray with your children, and pray with them until they are free from the fear. Pray Scriptures with your children. The enemy has no weapons that can stand against the word of God. One of our favourites is from Psalm 32:7: 'You are my hiding place, you always fill my heart with songs of deliverance and when I am afraid, I will trust in you. Let the weak say I am strong in the strength of my God.' The more I have filled my heart with the word of God, the more that word instantly comes to my aid in times of need. I have found those 'songs of deliverance' in my heart and in my mind whenever I have faced situations where I needed help, an answer, comfort, encouragement, courage or an idea of how to behave. And now our children are beginning to 'find' the word of God, which is so perfect that it seems tailor-made for what they are going through.

Anger

We know a family where the son had a problem with anger and with getting angry. The parents prayed and prayed, and they had others pray for their son too. They found a book written by a Christian author, which showed stages of dealing with anger, and taught youngsters how to express anger in appropriate and mature ways. They learned as much as they could about anger from Scripture. The Bible does not say, 'Do not get angry' but it does say, 'In your anger do not sin' (Ephesians 4:26). The parents kept on giving their son feedback. They would say things like, 'You are learning to express anger in better ways'; they would thank God when there was evidence of their boy's overcoming strong anger in his life. They began to find the roots of his aggression, i.e. what it was caused by, and they began to pray with their son for the Lord's healing in his life.

The parents were ready to persevere and to stand with their son 'for as long as it takes'.

Health

In another family we know, the eldest son was plagued by ear and sinus infections, from babyhood. At age 2, he was on antibiotics ten times in one twelve-month period. The parents began to pray. They asked God to heal their son. It was a ten-year battle. Some years their son got a cold in September, which lasted until June. The Lord spoke to them about halfway through and said he was going to break the power of these infections in their son's life. So they continued to pray. Whenever there were opportunities to receive prayer for healing in their church meeting, they encouraged their son to respond. Today he is healed.

Those parents realised they then had two choices:

a. They could just put it down to growing up – he just got over it as he got older.
b. They could acknowledge God.

They have chosen this response; they have chosen to believe, 'This is God's healing for our son; it is by his power and his goodness and we thank and acknowledge God's love and care in our son's life.'

Interestingly enough, everything in our Christian life comes down to our choice. We can choose to believe that something happened by coincidence or we can choose to bless God for it. Even faith in God must be by faith.

Family Exercise: What are My Giants?

Have each family member write out one or two giants in their life on a piece of paper. Let each person take turns reading aloud what he or she has written. After each has read out his or her giants, let the rest of the family members add no more than one or two extras to the list. This can be a vulnerable time as we are sometimes blind to things in our own lives which are stumbling blocks to us. This needs to be done in an atmosphere of love and covering. Parents need to receive the insights of their children with humility rather than with strong negative reaction or denial. The Bible talks about submitting ourselves to one another in love and when it comes to spiritual growth, this includes our children.

Once everyone has their 'giants' listed on a piece of paper (in our family, we used 'giant-shaped' pieces of paper) stand those pieces of paper against something. Read together the words David used against Goliath as you proceed to shoot down your giants with elastic bands. (This can be fun; we laughed a lot while we were doing it, but that didn't lessen the prophetic impact it had on us as a family.) Then pray together, thanking God that with his help your giants can be overcome just as David's was.

Read the story of David and Goliath together and note with your children how the great and insurmountable obstacle (Goliath) became an opportunity for the unqualified, powerless shepherd boy David to be used by God to bring freedom and military victory to an entire nation. Wherever possible, apply these principles on an ongoing basis in your life and help your children to do the same.

God's Heroes

How to help our children to become all that God made them to be, to encourage and help them to not only achieve their potential but also to set them on a path towards fulfilment of their unique and wonderful God-given destiny.

God often chose the least likely, least heroic types of people and made them into heroes, sometimes by giving them special abilities. Other times, however, God chose people who had no special abilities, but they were people who simply believed his word and obeyed him. Sometimes God's heroes were people who had nothing but faith in him and love for him. Noel Richard's song 'Heroes' has inspired this chapter. It was written many years ago, but its message is forever relevant. Here are the words:

I watched my childhood heroes fight their battles on TV
I imagined I was like them in my playground army.
When I grew older and put aside my childish games.
There were different heroes but the feeling was the same.
Though I tried to imitate them; to be famous of course.
Now I want to be one of God's heroes
And I'm not looking for applause.

I've made up my mind. I wanna be one of your heroes.
To live or die for you because I love you so.
I kneel at your feet and I promise my allegiance.
Though you may be the only one who knows.

I may not be a great hero, Lord I know they're rare and few.
But if there's nothing you want of me, just to be your friend
    will do.
Yet I am always ready and I am willing to be trained
If I can serve your purpose, if just one life I can change.
And if that person is a hero and causes men to follow you.
I will know that it was worth it all
To be a nobody for you.

I have a goal before me, I will pursue my dream.
That in ordinary people, your love will be revealed.
O yes I have ambition, to be a hero for you Lord.
I want to do what you are asking, so that strength in me is
    formed.
I know I'm not a special person, I'm just a gatherer of songs.
Yet in my heart there is a longing
To see your will on earth be done.

Words: Noel Richards and Gerald Coates. Music: Noel Richards
© 1986 Sovereign Lifestyle Music Ltd

- Let's continue in prayer for our children, from birth if possible – prayer for their lives, that God's wonderful and unique plan for each will be fulfilled. Parents can call in their children's destiny and can speak in faith over their children while they are asleep, that 'this child fulfil God's purposes' in his or her life.

- Let's ask God to rekindle our own passion for Jesus, which like a perfume we wear, will naturally rub off on our children. It is Jesus we aim to please, him we serve and his reward we look for rather than to achieve importance, fame or status. We can teach our children through the experiences of everyday living that to be famous in man's eyes is temporal; it doesn't last, but to be known and loved by God is eternal. We can encourage our children to live out a life filled with the pursuit of God rather than the pursuit of fame, significance or riches if we ourselves model this radical lifestyle.

- We can talk about Bible heroes, especially when your child's situation is 'a bit like what happened to Ruth or Esther, or Daniel or Joshua'. Wherever possible, earth your child's experiences in Scripture. This means to tell your children when what they are experiencing is 'just like what happened to David – he felt very sad too', or 'just like what happened to Thomas – he doubted too'. It will make the Scriptures come alive to them. Earth your family's experiences in Scripture.

- If you mean to trust God and if you decide to go through your troubles living by faith, if you have godly friendships and good people praying for you and praying with you, then it can be very positive to share your troubles and problems with your children in a way that is appropriate to their age. Share the difficulties you face. If your children can live through an experience with you rather than just hear about something you have faced, then no sceptic in later years can argue away a truth about the Christian faith. Your children will know the truth because they have lived it.

Example:

One family we know had gone through a particularly hard time and had been faced with a great deal of stress and anxiety. They shared these experiences with their children; they prayed together and they chose to trust God together. Each time God did a miracle in their lives, they rejoiced together. One day they called together a number of friends; it was Father's Day and the family wanted to publicly bless their Father God and declare in front of their friends and in front of all

Heaven, the goodness and faithfulness of God. All of their children, aged 11, 13 and 15, spoke publicly in front of their friends. Their 15-year-old son said the following: 'For the past two years I have tried out this life of faith to see when it would fall down, when it wouldn't work. It never happened. God has always saved us through all the trouble we've been through, God has never let us fall, he has never let go of us.'

- You may have had times of doubt and fear, but Jesus' love and faithfulness is solid as a great rock through any situation. Nothing you have faced or will face is a surprise or a worry to Jesus. The greatest example any parent can set for their children is not to be perfect in faith or strength or courage, but to know where to find refuge and to know where to find perfect peace and strength. We can do nothing greater than to turn to Jesus when facing our seemingly insurmountable obstacles. If we lean on Jesus, then as surely as day follows night, we will experience the same miracle Moses did when facing a great and impassable sea; we can stand with our children, 'stand firm and you will see the deliverance the Lord will bring you today' (Exodus 14:13) in our own lives.

- We can continue, as parents, to make the most of every opportunity in the most natural of settings to bring out key lessons to be learned from Bible heroes. Following is an example from a family we know. The names are fictitious but the events are true.

Example:

Both Jack and Susan lost their jobs on the same day. Jack's company had gone bust and because he had a position of authority in the company, he faced a major court battle, where they stood to lose the family house.

There had been injustice in their job situation, and the Lord had given them Psalm 124 to Psalm 126, saying he would miraculously deliver them. Throughout 17 months of unemployment, Jack and Susan and the family never lacked for anything. God provided them with food, money through the letterbox, even chocolates for the children on Valentine's Day, and money, specifically marked 'meal out money' on the eve of their wedding anniversary. To Jack and Susan's knowledge, no one knew of their special day.

The family decided to trust in God's word together, in the face of a bankruptcy petition, where they had no money to find a solicitor and no hope of receiving legal aid. They had an evening of spontaneous intercession, where they literally stood together on all the words God had given them. During this evening they worshipped together, they wrote the word 'Fear' on a piece of paper – one of the children crumpled the paper up and threw it out the door, shouting, 'Fear, you get out of our lives.'

The family did receive legal aid against all odds. The aid came through in 26 hours rather than weeks, as the solicitor had advised would happen in the best scenario. The court case was settled out of court, there was no bankruptcy and the Lord brought great vision and calling into all their lives through this time. New direction came and many divine appointments and connections occurred.

At some of the darkest times, the family had a feast together, because the Bible says, 'You prepare a table before me in the presence of my enemies.' They chose to rejoice in the Lord despite their natural circumstances and despite their feelings. Throughout this time, their children prayed with them, prophesied over them, and trusted God with them. Their teenage son received no pocket money for the full 17 months, but never complained. During that time, he was miraculously, and from different sources, given all the things he had hoped to buy with his pocket money.

During this time, when no money was available for clothes or books or gifts, the children's shoes didn't wear out and their feet didn't grow out of their shoes. The family had decided at the outset, just as they had lost their jobs, to never go to people with their needs. If they were out of money and had a need they prayed, and practised trusting the Lord to provide. One day, a financial gift for a specific debt came in the post within one hour of their prayer.

Trusting God

Following are practical suggestions for helping children to trust God in reality and not as a religious statement, which means nothing. If this is your desire, and if you dare to ask God to help you teach your children to trust, you will most certainly come upon difficult circumstances.

I will never forget the time we were facing great difficulty in our small business venture and I kept asking, 'Lord, why are things so difficult, why do we have to face such giant problems?' The Lord's response was immediate: 'What song did you sing over and over, literally dozens of times, many years ago?' The words to the song came blazing across my mind:

> O for a faith that will not shrink when pressed by many a foe
> That will not tremble on the brink of poverty or woe
> That will not mumble nor complain, beneath life's chastening rod
> But in the hour of grief or pain, will lean upon its God.

> (W. H. Bathurst)

I learned an indisputable and immutable truth that day that has made the years that followed easier – and harder. Faith is learned through desperate situations where only faith will get us through. Faith does not grow where it is not tested and stretched to where we think something will snap! Without the direst of situations, when there seems to be no way through the deepest, darkest valley, how will we ever see and experience the mighty deliverance and the glory of the awesome God of all Creation?

A challenge to parents: Have you ever seen the hand of God reach right into your circumstances and literally pull you out of deep waters the second before those waters closed over your head? These incredible experiences must be shared with our children so that they too can see God's mighty hand just like the literal children of Israel saw the pillar of fire and the cloud and the parting of the Red Sea. Those children were not spared the terrible sights of the abuses their people received at the hands of the Egyptians; they saw the Egyptian chariots pursuing them until their backs were to the sea. But the story of their deliverance has lasted and has been told and re-enacted every year for the past 4000.

And for us too, our business was saved eight years ago by a miracle that is still hard to believe and is still talked about.

Whenever something happens to you as a parent, in your job or your relationships, where you recognise your need to trust God, share it with your children. It may be inappropriate to share all the details in depth, but there is surely something of your journey of trust you can share. One way children learn is by modelling adult behaviour and if they see your walk of trust, they will surely learn to live in the same way.

- It follows that whenever things come up in your children's lives, which you may recognise as an opportunity for them to trust in God, you can help them to see their situation in a different way. Help them to see the problem or situation and its natural outcome, but then to see what

God is saying, how I can get through, what will I do (i.e. trust God). The conclusions we may come to due to society's perception of our problem and its natural outcome may be very different to the conclusions we may come to as a result of communication with and trust in God and his word. For example, our natural circumstances may say: 'Dad or Mum doesn't earn enough money for us to give anything away,' whether to our local church or to charities. To trust God is to give as God asks and to believe that he will provide for our needs.

- Find the word of God for your own situation (the Bible is the first place to look) and help your children find the word of God in theirs. Put specific Bible verses up somewhere in your home where they are visible and where all can see them, read them and believe them! Read God's word aloud with your children and together speak out your choice to trust it. Declare that you are putting your trust in God rather than in people or your own expertise or experience (though God may use these things). See what happens!

- Learn to treasure the word of God in your own life; your children will learn to do the same. Value the living word of God on a daily basis, both as you read it in the Bible and as you hear from the Lord in your own heart. Learn to welcome God's personal words to you as they apply to the unique circumstances and situations you face. Apply the word of God in your children's lives too.

Example:

We know a family whose young teenage daughter is learning to love the word of God and to value it in her own life. Why? Because she is realising the powerful way God's word in Scripture speaks into her situation and

149

applies to her life time and time again. But this didn't happen automatically. She has been brought up on a diet of the importance of Scripture, from a young child, even before she went to school. As soon as she could read she was given her own Bible and the parents read it with her as often as they could. As she grew older, they encouraged her to read her Bible for herself, as often as she was able. They encouraged her to make a note of Scriptures through which God spoke to her. They encouraged her and blessed God together when she shared instances where God spoke to her through the Bible. Sometimes God spoke to her directly into her heart, or through a life situation. The parents gave her strong encouragement at these times too.

- Sometimes our children trust us and we betray that trust. These times are a wonderful opportunity not only to ask for forgiveness from our children, but also to teach them that there is One who is totally trustworthy and who will never betray their trust. Thank God together for his faithfulness, which is endless.

- In a difficult situation, it is easy to get bogged down with the pain of it all and hard to focus our attention on anything else. But the Bible says to look to God, and situations where trust is required give us a wonderful opportunity to practise focusing on God and his purposes rather than on our immediate circumstances. We spend a great deal of energy feeling very anxious and worried when we look at our frightening circumstances. How much better to focus on Jesus, who totally transcends our situation, who has more strength and grace to clothe us with, than we will ever need. There is only one way to learn to focus on Jesus, simply by practice. How many times have we looked at difficult situations and circumstances as God's grace and kindness in our lives? He knows it is only by *practice* that we can learn to trust. It is sometimes only when we are desperate that we will focus on Jesus. Is it possible that God our Father is gracious and loving enough to lead us right into the face of danger for precisely this purpose?

Scriptures about Trust

Psalm 9:10; Proverbs 3:5-6; Jeremiah 17:5-8; Isaiah 26:3-4; John 14:1; Matthew 14:22-33. Share these with your children, get the children to read them, you read them aloud, give your children rewards for memorising some of them, put them up on fridges and notice boards, and so on.

• It may be that you 'blow it'; that you have a perfect opportunity to trust God and you don't. How important it is to share it with your children and to let them see by your own example that it is never too late to begin to trust God again. There is no failure that is too great that we cannot turn around and begin to trust God once again.

The Armour of God

Helping children to see the battle they are engaged in and then to be prepared each day. Giving your children the keys to understanding God's protection, which is available for them. Teaching your children to use the 'weapons of our warfare' in an effective way.

- Teach your children about the battle you are in together. Pray that God will give you his strategy for your children. Pray over your children's beds and over their clothes. Pray protection. Pray anointing. Pray they are set on fire with a passion for Jesus. Regularly declare God's purposes (as found in Scripture and from prophetic words you may have had) over your children. Understand that out of a passion for Jesus often comes a passion for the lost, for the poor and for justice. Realise that if you are yielding your children up to God's purposes, you are preparing them to go where he takes them.

- Literally cover your children with Scripture. We covered an old sheet with Scriptures about the Lord's ability to deliver us from fear. We covered one of our children with it for a number of months before she went to sleep. From that point on, our child stopped exhibiting strong and irrational fear. She began to deal with fear through prayer and standing on God's word. We could see the progress she was making and told her so. We taught our child that the word of God has power. We prophetically enacted what we believed. While literally covering her with the word of God, we spoke out that God's word has power to deliver us from all fear. But more than just speaking out a bunch of words, we actually believed what we spoke out, and we believed God would move and would display his power as a result of our declaration of faith. He did. The word of God covered our child spiritually just as it did physically. It was a physical action to display, to underline, to highlight, a spiritual truth.

- Realise that you as a parent have such a significant role in helping your children find their destiny in God. The enemy prefers passive parents because he so desperately fears the power of praying parents. Take up your own weapons and your God-given place of prayer and practical support in order to truly stand with your children. Our children have great need of our prayers, our warfare, our encouragement, our faith, our wisdom and our experience. For us to do nothing would be devastating. God help us to pray consistently, confidently and fervently for our own children and to use all the spiritual resources at our disposal to cover the emerging generations with powerful and effective prayer. This is our destiny and this is their destiny. It will not just fall into our laps; we need to take hold of it.

- Remember too that our enemy is real; he not only knows the potential of the young people of this generation but also has a clear, defined strategy to systematically destroy individuals in body, mind and spirit. Our children were born into a battle: a battle for their very existence and calling. Let's make no mistake, our children are on the enemy's hit list. It is not a question of whether or not we choose to enter that battle. It is raging around your children and mine as we speak. There are agendas, battle plans and objectives against our children and youth. The question is: will we or will we not give them the strategy, the weapons and the armour they need to stand and advance in this battle? To do nothing is to set them up for defeat.

- What about the children who have no Christian parents? What about the children who have never heard the gospel? Who will pray for them? What about the victims of child molestation? Who has prayed specifically for those children the enemy has targeted to be in the wrong place at the wrong time, to suffer abduction and even death? Here is a challenge and a strong encouragement to parents. You can pray these children right into the kingdom of God. Your prayers can defeat the enemy's plans in their lives too. You can cover in prayer the enemy's potential victims of such things as child abuse, you can pray creatively for the Lord's deliverance in their lives before such horrors occur. You can pray for God's mercy on perpetrators of abuse, and pray in the help those individuals need before they offend. You can pray with all the inspiration and creativity and power of God the Holy Spirit, knowing you are praying according to the will of God and knowing you are praying that God's will is done on earth.

- Roger and Sue Mitchell, who live in London, UK, and carry an amazing vision called Target Europe, give a wonderful picture of children going forth in the power of God, winning battles and demolishing strongholds. The second part of the picture is even more amazing: parents and guardians at home on their faces, literally crying out to God and interceding on behalf of their children. In the picture, the children have such great success, much of it because of their parents' intercession. What a powerful partnership across the generations!

- Ask God to help you to recognise enemy attack and deal with it either on your own in prayer, or standing together with other Christian friends, or with your child, where appropriate.

Example:

Another example from the world of bullying. An 8-year-old was being bullied and laughed at. His appearance was made fun of and he was laughed at during sports lessons, when he sometimes came last in races or couldn't catch balls very well. The result was that his self-esteem and self-confidence was being destroyed and his relationships were suffering. During PE lessons and sports activities, he began to not try any more because he felt he was no good. The parents began to realise that this was a spiritual battle to rob their child of what God had for him, to isolate him and render him ineffective as a Christian. The parents and their son prayed for the others who had been bothering him. They also prayed for appreciation to come into the classroom, where children's differences would be celebrated. They prayed against comparison and competition and prayed for acceptance of others to be the major influence. With their son, the parents looked for, and thanked God for, every evidence of his presence in the situation. As a result of prayer, the parents spoke to the teacher who told them that their son was actually average in sports and not poor at all. The truth went a long way to restore shaken self-confidence. The truth cut across the passivity and gave the child the confidence to once again try his best at sports. Soon he was on the school netball team, not the best player by any means, but totally enjoying himself and his friendships on the team. And, two years later, the child who had bullied him the most became his good friend. The two boys even began to have conversations about the love of God and the reality of Jesus.

- The armour of God is very strategically placed and covers us where we most need it. Are there situations in your child's life where his or her faith is attacked? Does your child ever experience accusing or condemning thoughts? Does your child ever get tempted to anger or jealousy, or tempted to behave in an unrighteous manner? Is your child ever tempted to believe a lie about himself or herself? In these times specific parts of the armour of God will come in very handy. Help your child to be clothed with the armour of God. For example: *You're believing a lie today – you are not stupid – God made you with these special gifts and abilities – remember your belt of truth – today you need to wear it.* You could even give your child a real belt to wear as a reminder of the truth in their life.

- Note that nearly everything in the armour of God as pictured in Ephesians 6 is for our defence to enable us to stand in battle. The only offensive weapon we have is the sword of the Spirit, which is the word of God. Remember to use the sword of the Spirit with your children whenever there is battle around. What does God's word say about this situation? What has Jesus got to say?

What does God's word say about my safety and my authority in this situation?

- Use Scriptures specific to your own situation – Scriptures which speak of the ground on which we stand and Scriptures which speak of our place in Jesus. Some examples are:

Psalm 18
Psalm 23
Isaiah 54:13,17
2 Corinthians 10:3-5; 12:9
Psalm 27
Psalm 91
Hebrews 12:2-3
2 Timothy 4:18
Romans 8:38

Faith, Worry and the Bread of Life

*Three themes are covered here. Building **faith** in our children on a day-to-day basis. Jesus said that people would not live by bread alone, but by every word that comes out of the mouth of God (Isaiah 40:3; Matthew 4:4) so following are ways of helping our children to feed on the **word of God** on a daily basis. Finally, ways of modelling a **lifestyle of trust** at all times, but especially in times of trouble or anxiety.*

- Take one of the following titles or themes each week. Take time with the children during the week (perhaps five minutes per day) to worship and note together something in their life or something that happened today which related to the specific title or theme. For example, if your theme for the week is God's Love, note his love for you or for someone else each day. Work towards everyone in the family eventually being able to do the same.

Themes

What God is doing today
God's love
God's provision for all my needs
God's goodness
God's plans for my life today

What God is saying to me today
God's presence – God is with me today
Let me welcome him into my life
What I can thank God for
Where I see evidence of God today
and so on.

Note: Do not feel guilty if you feel overwhelmed by a lot of ideas. Let God lead you. Do not religiously do one theme each day. Let God lead you. You may only end up doing one theme in a month. Praise God! Let these ideas inspire you and never condemn you. Let this imparting of the kingdom of God to your children be a delightful journey. Let these ideas release you into being the parent after God's own heart that he always envisioned.

- Practise feeding on the word of God each day, with your children. Thank God for his word. Pray for God to bring his word to life for you and your children and to speak into your hearts. Pray that God will show you and your children how his word applies to your situation.

  The Bible says: 'You are my hiding place; you always fill my heart with songs of deliverance and when I am afraid I will trust in you. Let the weak say, "I am strong in the strength of my Lord"' Psalm 32:7. I have found this passage to be literally true in my own life, simply because the Holy Spirit always brings to mind a Scripture which completely fits any situation I have found myself in. Sometimes I have woken up with a Scripture or words to a song based on Scripture and realised that the words have filled my mind all night. Always the words are an amazing encouragement from heaven straight into whatever I am facing. I share these things to excite and inspire parents, because this is exactly the kind of daily encouragement and help God our Father wants to give everyone who looks for it and who will receive it.

We cannot do better than to literally 'get Scripture into our children'; into their hearts, their minds and their Spirits so that they too can experience the Holy Spirit filling their hearts with 'songs of deliverance' for every situation they will face.

Example:

I remember the daughter of a friend of mine who was facing a very difficult time in her secondary school. She was feeling unhappy there and was fearful of many of her peers. She wondered if she made a mistake in choosing the school she was at and whether she should move away. She prayed over her situation with her mother and later on said, 'I believe God has told me to read Psalm 3:6.' When together they opened the Bible and read the words, they were thrilled to find that the words not only exactly fitted the daughter's situation, but also gave her direction as to what to do. She stayed at that school and today, at age 13, leads a prayer group comprising students from a number of different churches, which prays for the school two mornings a week.

- Read the Bible to your children. Read just a part of a sentence first. Speak out phrases from the Bible and reward your children for learning them, which will often happen quite spontaneously, just by them copying you. Friends of the Australia Children's Prayer Network have challenged me because their children know long passages of Scripture off by heart. It is incredible to listen to young children speaking straight from the Bible words of such wisdom and power, beauty and magnitude.

- Sing phrases or verses from the Bible to your children and encourage them to do the same. Practise singing to the Lord in your own home in English, or sing in tongues on your own or to classical music, jazz or other instrumental rhythms. Be free and experiment often with singing to the Lord. Experiment with your children. Don't be shy to sing to the Lord in English or in tongues when your children are around. Don't try to hide your love for Jesus from your children; it is the most valuable thing you have to share with them. It will be your most precious legacy.

- Make colourful posters of Scripture verses and put them up in prominent places in your home for a season, where everyone can't help but read a particular verse over and over again.

- Pray for your children, that God will give them such a love for his word; that they will see the Bible for the great treasure house that it is. Pray that the Lord will give them such a hunger for his word, that they will be drawn to it.

- Have family times reading the Bible stories together, where everyone takes turns reading. Allow your children to ask questions and discuss together what you have read.

- Prophetically enact various Scriptures.

  Example:

  Once as a family we were at a place of transition in our lives and God spoke this word to us, through a song called 'Every Place' by Dave Bilborough (1997, Kingsway's Thankyou Music). The song spoke about the Lord having already given us every place we put the sole of our foot down upon – and that the Lord's promises would never fail or forsake us.' We looked the words up in the Bible – Joshua 1:3-5 – and realised that the Lord was giving these promises to us in our own life situation. We immediately wrote down on separate pieces of paper all the areas of our lives that were currently being contended. We wrote down our dreams as well as words spoken over us regarding God's purposes for our lives and for our future. We danced on them, we walked on them as if what was written was territory. God said, 'I will give you every place where you set your foot, as I have promised Moses' (Joshua 1:3) and 'No one will be able to stand against you' (Joshua 1:5). So we stepped all over these papers. Many things were accomplished that day:

Our faith grew tremendously; it actually felt like a momentous occasion. We were acting out believing God's word in front of all spiritual forces in heaven and on earth.
We were literally stepping into our destiny.
We were responding to God.

- As children get older, you can give them rewards for learning Bible phrases to start with and then Bible verses. Children love charts where they can earn a star or a sweet or some coins each time they learn a verse.

- There are countless ways to encourage learning Bible verses. Why not do a family challenge with older children or teens? Everyone can contribute some money towards the final prize, which one person wins, after having memorised the most Bible verses in a given time.

- Always relate the word of God to your daily life. Tell your children what God's word says for your present situation or circumstances. Share God's specific words to you with your children. For example, one morning I woke up after having had a terrible nightmare, all to do with our children and their future. I knew it was just a dream, but it left me feeling devastated, a feeling I couldn't shake. I went to the word of God and simply began to look up Scriptures, which were God's promises to us for our children, Scriptures that the Lord had given us over the years. As I read the Scriptures aloud, I was astounded at how quickly the oppressive feelings simply disappeared. Today I cannot even remember the dream. Of course we shared this with our children and they are now able to deal with nightmares in similar ways.

- Illustrate the Bible with your children. As they draw pictures and do various forms of art, encourage them to create art based on the Bible and upon Bible stories. Make collages of faith words, or descriptions of God or of Jesus, or of Noah's animals or paintings illustrating Bible themes, such as God's love or giving.

- Throughout life, there will be times when children worry or are anxious. Practise laying aside habitual passive worrying, which can almost be an involuntary reaction to a difficult situation. Practise replacing the worry with an active declaration of God's word. As you and your children practise the latter, faith will become habitual. You may be amazed at the transformation in your family's life.

The House on the Rock

We have interpreted this Bible passage as Jesus talking about putting his words into practice and what fruit there would be in our lives as a result of that. We did not look at the Scriptures from the perspective of building our lives on Jesus as a foundation.

Therefore, helping your children put Jesus' words into practice in their everyday lives.

- As you read particularly the Gospels with your children, you will come across many words Jesus spoke. You may decide to take a different Scripture each week and ask your child: 'How can we put this into practice and make it a part of our lives?' Decide together what you might do or what you might change in your home.

- As you pray with your children, ask God to put his word inside you – ask the Lord to change you on the inside. God's word is very powerful, Timothy tells us, and we can say 'Yes' to God's word in our lives. You can say with your children, 'Yes, Lord, we want your word to have an effect in our lives.'

- Ask God to give you and your children a love for his word – a love for the Bible.

- Set aside time each day to read the Bible with your children (you could read simple Bible story books with very young children but you could also read them one simple Bible verse each day, which you may have paraphrased or put into their language).

- When you have your own times of prayer and you pray for your children, ask the Lord to give them an understanding of his word by revelation and beyond their years.

- Sleep on the word of God. Put a favourite Scripture, or one that is particularly relevant for you or your children, under their pillow or under your own pillow. The Scripture can be an encouraging one to highlight God's love, his protection, his promises to counter fear, or simply something about the nature of God. For example, if your child is afraid of the dark or has a spate of bad dreams, write out Psalm 4:8 on a sheet of card and put that under his or her pillow. It is a practical act of faith and a way of declaring: 'I believe this and I am living by it.' But it is also a prophetic act and will therefore affect the physical situation. As another example, if your child does not have a father or has lost his or her father, or has had problems with an inappropriate or difficult father, you could place Scriptures about the Father heart of God under your child's pillow. This action could be alongside your own fervent prayers that God as Father will touch your child and be a Father to him or her – that your child can know God as Father.

The Lost Sheep

Helping our children:

- *to understand the meaning of being lost*
- *to receive God's own heart and passion for the lost*
- *to understand the true nature of world mission and our part in the Great Commission.*

This is a risky business; if we want to follow Jesus with all our hearts, it will cost us everything. We need to be willing for God to touch our children in ways we have not imagined, in ways that could well be a profound challenge to us.

- Pray often for yourself and for your children, that God will give you his heart for the lost.

  Example:

  We know a new Christian, a person who has only known Jesus for a short time. He has had virtually no training or Bible reading. He has hardly attended a Christian church due to his life circumstances. But his heart is broken for those people who don't know Jesus and wherever he goes, he reaches out to the lonely, the hurting, the sad. His heart beats with passion for people around the world, people from every nation. He hasn't learned about the lost, or the harvest, or read Scriptures about the Great Commission. He hasn't mustered up these feelings because he has seen Christians with the same passion or because he thought he should. He cannot help how he feels. It is obvious to us that this man has simply been given part of God's own heart for a lost creation. God is able to give us his heart too.

• In these days, perhaps for the first time in human history, when the possibility of world evangelisation is no longer a far-fetched dream, how do we as a family respond? What is God asking of us? Read the Great Commission with your children (Matthew 28:16-20) and pray that God would help you as a family and as individuals respond to his word. You might simply feel that you should begin to pray together for a neighbour and ask God for opportunities to serve and bless that person as well as opportunities to share Jesus with them.

• As we are bombarded with local, national and global issues of poverty, injustice, homelessness, war, famine and disease, what is God asking of us? Make this an issue for prayer as a family. There will be a unique response that you can make, but teach your children to respond to Jesus and not be filled with condemnation or guilt on the basis of what others are doing or not doing. The truth is that there are issues on our own doorsteps, where God is calling Christians to make a difference. A mission field can be as near as your own street, it can be a people group in your own community just as easily as a people group far away. We have two friends who are called to the Muslim world, one to an African nation and the other to her own community. The callings are equally of

God, the people are equally gifted and anointed for the task. The person called to Africa is investing in individuals and building relationships which will take years; he is ploughing a hard ground and sowing seeds in desperately dry soil and he recognises that there will be no quick fix. The person called to the Muslim world in her own community is inundated with opportunities to share her faith and is seeing far more openness to the gospel by a greater number of people in a much shorter time.

- Save encouraging stories and share them with your children. For example, Cheri Fuller shares a true story in her wonderful book *When Children Pray* (Multnomah Publishers, 1998). Some of the following is adapted from that book and used by permission. A 9-year-old girl called Hope was researching the country of Mongolia as part of a school assignment. Hope was shocked and saddened to note that in Mongolia the vast majority of the people had Buddhist altars in their homes; and there were very few Bibles. Hope decided to pray – every day – that God would replace the Buddhist altars with Bibles. After faithfully praying for Mongolia and for its people for two years Hope came across an article in a missions magazine. The article stated that there had just been a revival in Mongolia and 500 people became followers of Jesus. Incredibly, that article was entitled, 'Hope for Mongolia'! How good is our God! During the next year, the Mongolian believers grew from 500 to 1000 and started Mongolia's first church. They called that church 'Hope Assembly'. At that time no one knew of Hope's faithful prayers – except Jesus. And today, a number of years later, this amazing story continues. There are some 165 churches in Mongolia according to

Walter Heidenreich from Ludenscheid, Germany. Walter and his team met with Christians from Mongolian churches at the History Maker Conference in June 2002. Every day they saw people healed and saved and many signs and wonders.

- Continually find ways to be thankful. Thank God for salvation, that you as a family are followers of Jesus. Teach your children to acknowledge God in every life situation they face. We have a far higher calling than to live by luck or to believe in coincidence. Find ways as a family to thank God, when you recognise his help or his intervention. Learn to recognise God at work in your family more and more.

- Pray for yourself and for your children, especially if you are providing a Christian home environment. Many churchgoing young people and young adults who've been brought up in a Christian home find it difficult to walk with Jesus, because they feel they haven't been saved out of a terrible life. They've not had a horrific past or needed great deliverance. They have been Christian for as long as they can remember. Sometimes, these young people haven't experienced the joy of being saved out of darkness or bondage or a hopeless situation. The truth is that we all need an understanding from God – or a revelation – of what it is to be lost. The truth is that there are not degrees of being lost; whether you've been on drugs or living in the gutter doesn't make you more lost than a person growing up in a loving Christian home. Jesus made this very clear to Nicodemus, who had followed the law with all his heart from his childhood (John 3). Lost is lost! The gap between being lost and saved is immeasurably greater than the gap between having lived a rebellious life (in terms of how we see 'rebellion') and a non-rebellious one. The Bible clearly states that all have sinned and that all our acts of righteousness are like filthy rags when compared to God's standards of righteousness. Every one of us needs saving just as much as the worst evildoer we can imagine. Pray for your children, particularly when you feel they reach the age of accountability, that God will show them a revelation of what it is to be lost – and what they too have been saved from. Pray that God in his mercy will give your children a true heart understanding of the wonder of salvation for them personally.

- Rejoice together as a family when someone you know becomes a Christian.

- Practise intercession for the lost. As a simple example, one family we know put on a tape recording of a song by Noel and Tricia Richards called 'For all the people who live on the earth' (1994, Kingsway's Thankyou Music). They listened to this song while on their knees, letting the words to the song become their prayer for the lost. The Spirit of God came down in that home, one of the children was in tears, groaning and praying for 'the people who don't know Jesus'.

- I refer again to a wonderful book to read together as a family, called *Window on the World* by Daphne Spraggett with Jill Johnstone (Angus Hudson Ltd, 2001).

- Buy a globe or a map of the world and pray with your children for the people in different countries. Ask God to lead and guide you in prayer and in terms of action. You may find that God gives your child a heart for a particular country. Help your child to learn about that country and to pray for the country and its people.

- Get involved in your church mission programme in some way. Get to know people who are working in other countries and hear their passionate hearts. Hear from God as to practical, prayer and financial ways to support the mission focus of your own church community.

- Spend time with and talk with and listen to people who have been called either for a short season or for many years to another nation or a specific people group within their own nation. Let their heart for the lost rub off on you and your children.

- Realise that there may be consequences of being open as a family to God's heart for those who do not have a saving faith in Jesus. One family we know has had to allow and support their children in a desire to learn different languages in preparation for their future. Those children have developed a heart for two different nations and a desire to go and share the gospel with people there.

- Understand that we as Christians are a mission people; there is no mission field that is greater than another. It is totally untrue that people who go to another nation are greater in God's eyes than people who never go abroad. In fact, the author would like to suggest that those people who stay behind and support the missionaries by heartfelt prayer, by financial support and by giving of their time to administer various things, are just as necessary, just as valuable to God and just as important.

The question is not: Are we called to be missionaries? The question for every family to respond to is: Where has Jesus called *us* to go? To whom are *we* called? Where is *our* mission field?

Potter and Clay

Helping our children to learn to yield to God the Holy Spirit as he faithfully and consistently works his wonder in their young lives. Helping our children to understand the Father heart of God and not only to learn of his desire for the best for them in every circumstance but also to understand his complete ability to mould and shape them into a beautiful and unique creation. How to instil in your children a trust that God has a unique and special purpose for their life, which is unlike his purpose for any other. The fruit of this kind of understanding will be a tremendous personal security, which will stand strong and unshakeable through the storms of life.

- Have you as a parent ever felt yourself being moulded by God? Have you told your children, 'This is when God shaped and moulded me'? What has it felt like and what has happened when you have yielded to God? Have you ever resisted God's touch or his purposes? It would be so helpful to your children to hear about your personal experiences. It would not only bring reality to the things they have talked about and heard about but it would also be a great encouragement to their faith in God's involvement with them.

- Tell your child a story, complete with sitting in front of the fire (if you have one), or in a cosy place with a drink together. The story is all about how you met Jesus and just what he means to you.

- Have you as a parent experienced the Father heart of God for you? Pray for your children that they will quickly experience the same. Consciously receive the grace of God for every time you fail in your dealings with your children, asking and trusting him to cover your mistakes. Yield those weak areas of your own life to God as Father believing his word, which states that he is able to change and heal you (Philippians 1:6).

- With your children, visit a potter at work and watch how he or she moulds and shapes the clay. For example, when a piece of clay has impurities in it, a potter will roll and stretch that piece of clay out as far as it will go, right to breaking point, in order to get out all the impurities. This happens again and again, until all the imperfections are taken out of the clay. A pot made with these imperfections is weak, prone to cracking, and may not even make it through the firing process. Chat these things over with your children, and speak about God's work as potter in each of our lives.

- Talk to your children and tell them when you see God at work in their lives. Let them know that you see this as an opportunity for them to yield to God as the potter. Help them to see that yielding to God can be an exciting as well as a difficult time because we will come through changed for the better, new in some area, free in another, healed in another.

Jesus Calms the Storm

Cultivating a lifestyle of trust, based upon keeping our eyes on Jesus and not upon our situation. We can be sure beyond doubt that our children will face trouble and difficulty in their lives on countless occasions. There is nothing material we can give them that can even be compared to the benefits of the art of trusting Jesus through thick and thin.

- Storms in life are inevitable and while we often pray for God to 'get us out of this storm', or 'take this storm away', God's best is often to show his power and glory by taking us safely *through* the storm.

- Encourage your children to call on Jesus in every situation; to look to Jesus first. Is our first response to a difficult situation panic, anxiety, negative confession, fear, passivity, or rushing to do something in our own strength, or are we in the habit of going to Jesus?

- As those storms, common to all family life – storms of sickness, accident, rows, financial worry, job-related problems – inevitably come our way, let's model our response to our children. Let them see that we take all that we face, whether good or bad, to Jesus. Let them see our praise and acknowledgement of God's hand in our every situation and let them see our turning first to Jesus in every time of difficulty.

- Let's share our troubles with our children, wherever it is appropriate. While it is unhelpful to burden our children beyond their years by sharing with them things they may truly not be able to understand or mentally deal with, there is surely something of our trials we can share with our children. Then they can pray through the problems with us; we may be surprised at and humbled by our children's faith and their God-given wisdom for our situation. Let us also not deny our children the priceless opportunities to see God's goodness and faithfulness and deliverance through difficulty. If we never share our troubles with them, they will not see the deliverance of God in the same way as if we just tell them about it after the fact.

- We can talk for years about God's peace, but the only way to know God's peace is to experience it. Thank God with your children for the storms in life; they are a precious opportunity to find a real refuge and a strong tower. They are a brilliant learning experience for your children, where they cannot only 'taste and see that the Lord is good', but where they can also experience the peace of God.

- The home should be a place of refuge for children, and not another place of warfare. All too often, we forget that children face so many battles during their day and children who are followers of Jesus are truly at the cutting edge of their 'society'. They are truly on the front lines and in the thick of the battle. We are sometimes too quick to lash out at our children after our own bad day, forgetting that this home is their primary place of refuge. God help us to cultivate a loving relationship with our children, where even times of discipline are saturated with the presence of Jesus.

- Let's intercede regularly for our children; it is a powerful way for parents to stand with their children as they are sent out each day. Let's pray for God's protection on their minds and hearts and bodies. Let's pray for the presence of Jesus to surround them and for them to personally experience that 'friend who is closer than a brother' through their times of difficulty.

- Let's encourage our children to talk to Jesus during their day, even if it's just a 'Thank you, Lord' or a 'Help, Jesus, now what do I do?'

- A challenge to all parents. Jesus said, 'All authority in heaven and on earth is given to me' (Matthew 28). To me, that statement means that Jesus has power over *all* storms. As a parent, do you and I believe this? If we believe this by faith and actually live it, the results will speak volumes in the lives of our children and will arm them mightily for all the unbelief and scepticism they will face. No one will be able to tell them that God is not real – *they will know different because they have lived it!*

Spiritual First Aid Box

Helping our children to live by the word of God and giving them practical tools to enable them to gain a first-hand knowledge of Scripture. A spiritual first aid box is simply a box of Scripture verses filed under various categories, such as: Verses about Jesus, Verses about Faith, Verses about Fear, and so on.

- Encourage your child to use their first aid box regularly
  Every day
  In every situation where help is needed.

- Explain to your children that in today's society, needing help is a sign of weakness and independence is perceived as a sign of maturity and strength. But God created us to be in relationship – to help and to be helped – to need him and one another. This is truly a sign of maturity and strength. Note 2 Corinthians 12:9-10 with your children.

- Help or encourage your children to add to their Spiritual First Aid Box as a need or a situation or a special Scripture arises. This will help to expand your and your child's knowledge of Scripture.

- Encourage your children to memorise Bible verses. The Bible says: *Your word is a lamp unto my feet* (Psalm 119:105). As we fill our lives with Scripture and put

God's word inside of us, the Holy Spirit files it some-where within and always brings it up in a situation or circumstance of need. How many have woken up with a Scripture verse or song flooding their mind, which is totally relevant or is God's wisdom or shows the way for a problem or situation they will be facing that day? Out of personal experience of many years, we can confi-dently say that there is a word from God for every situ-ation and it is amazing how the Holy Spirit brings it to mind. Our children can live like this.

- Read God's promises together; they are there for us to receive by faith and will have a life-changing effect on us. The effect of imbibing the promises of Scripture continues and grows over the years. Actively look for verses in the word of God, which speak into your own life situations. Actively look for encouragements in the word of God for your own family and for your own children's circumstances.

- Read the Bible together as a family, or listen to it on tape. Read in creative ways and act out different Bible stories. Let the children have turns to read to the rest of the family and give them space to expound on God's word – let your children practise telling you about what they've read. Encourage them to listen to God and share what he has shown them about what you've read. This is the beginning of preaching. Make the Bible such a part of your daily life that it becomes a life habit. As your children grow up, Bible reading will become a natural and expected part of each day. As they grow older, chil-dren can be encouraged to read their own Bible on a daily basis. Reward them for doing so. Have children illustrate what they've read. Let your children choose what to read on a given day. Find ways of bringing the Bible to life.

- Wherever possible, earth your children in Scripture. Whenever your child's situation reminds you of an event or character in the Bible, tell them so and explain why. For example: *'You're facing a situation just like King David did, when . . .'* or *'You remind me of Timothy in the Bible . . .'*

The Outward Appearance or the Heart

This theme is such a great challenge to parents because the home is a great place for reality. It is nearly impossible in the home to hide our true attitudes. As the following paraphrase of Jesus so aptly put it, 'The things that come out of the mouth come from the heart and these make you unclean' (Matthew 15:18-19). So some very practical and very challenging suggestions follow, to help us and our children allow God the Holy Spirit to: 'Create in me a pure heart O God' (Psalm 51:10).

- Have discussions with your children – discussions about our motivation for our speech and behaviour. Is our motivation pure? Are we speaking or acting as a faith response to Jesus? Or are we speaking or acting out of a desire for recognition, or fame, or approval, or fear of man, or jealousy, or wanting to get our own back? These are a few of many attitudes, which are not pure.

- In the home, during the course of everyday actions and reactions, there will be many times when parents can explain our individual responsibility before God. Each of us can learn to respond to Jesus instead of to the demands of our situation or to need or to emotional pressure. Tackle these situations with your children as they happen. Let your response to your child be out of an attitude of 'Let's explore this situation together, let's explore your feelings, let's understand why you are behaving this way.' Our children need to understand that they are on a journey of knowing God and that heart attitudes are part of the journey. Help your children to understand that heart attitudes are extremely important. This is something they do not always learn at school. As a supply teacher, I realise just how often teachers tell children, to 'be friends' or to 'say sorry'. Everyone knows that they don't have to mean it, because within the next five minutes they can be fighting again.

• Our children should never be made to feel that they are failures or are themselves unacceptable, or are displeasing us. We need to learn to tackle the issue of heart attitudes with our children, in the context of repentance and sanctification and not in the context of disapproval or punishment. In other words, repentance is a wonderful emotion, because it is a turning from sin and a turning to God. In terms of sanctification, Jesus is making us clean and making us new. ('If anyone is in Christ there is a new Creation, the old has gone, the new has come!' 2 Corinthians 5:17.) That should be an exciting and exhilarating prospect. The Lord himself is in us making us new, able to work in us to help us to 'will and to act according to his good purpose' (Philippians 2:13). The Bible is clear that the Lord is able to complete the good work he has begun in us (Philippians 1:6). We should never put our children under feelings of guilt or disapproval when they fail to display a godly attitude. They should never have to work to display a godly response on the surface just for fear of punishment, which so often can be the case on the school playground, where sincere and hardworking teachers have an incredibly difficult and challenging task.

- Pray with your children and open your hearts to God. Ask him to rule over your heart and to fill you with attitudes, which are pleasing to him, from the inside out.

- Remind your children of the twofold word in Philippians 2:12-13; that while God promises to work out his best in us, we are to also work out 'your own salvation'. This is exactly what we are doing as we yield our heart attitudes to God.

- Remind your children of Scriptures like Philippians 1:6 as an encouragement, that God is able to complete the good work he has begun in us.

- Remind your children of King David's prayer, when he cried out to God, 'Create in me a pure heart, O God' (Psalm 51:10). Pray this prayer with your children, fully expecting that God will answer.

- Remember that in the media, on TV and in magazines, the outward appearance is everything. The reality is that the most beautiful and successful looking person could be the most sinful and the sickest person inside. We can all think of many examples. The press, which loves and displays outward beauty on the one hand, is so quick to expose sickness of heart in the very superstars it helped to mould. This is in direct opposition to the kingdom, where the inward appearance or the heart attitude is everything. The poorest, least educated, least physically attractive person could be the purest in heart and therefore so beautiful to the Lord. The Bible so aptly puts it: God's ways are not our ways (Isaiah 55:8).

- The Bible (Luke 18:9-14) has a perfect story to illustrate this. It is the story of the Pharisee and the Tax Collector.

On the surface, the Pharisee looked totally justified before God, and even he believed that he was pure and upstanding. He actually believed he was better than others. He did not even see the pride in his heart, which God detested. On the other hand, all the tax collector could see was his need for God's mercy. He was a man who was outwardly despised because of the nature of his job, yet the Bible tells us that he went home justified before God. The Lord saw the humility and reality in his heart and blessed him.

- We need also to remember that in the world, our worth is based on what we do, in the kingdom, our worth is based on Jesus. Who we are becomes much more important than what we do. It is so important to help our children to understand these subtleties in our western culture. No wonder the Lord said we are to be in the world, but not of the world.

- You and I can impart the kingdom to our children by yielding to God in our own job.

  Example:

  In our business situation we were often tempted to do small things which were not quite honest but which nobody would know about. We knew God would know, and we had to choose to act rightly sometimes in the midst of strong criticism from business associates, who were pressing us into so-called grey areas. We are often called upon to do small things that we know are wrong; others justify these things by saying, 'C'mon, it won't harm anybody, it's just a tiny thing.' It is precisely because the Lord sees our hearts that the choices we make will affect our lives and our futures. These choices will therefore also affect our children and our witness to them.

Garments of Praise
Helping our children to develop a lifestyle of praise.

- Find out what the Bible says about praise. Psalms are a good place to start, though the Old and New Testaments are rich with teaching on and examples of praise. Learn about praise with your child and creatively put into practice what you have learned. God has made us all creative people because he has made us all in his image. With the Holy Spirit to inspire us to creativity, what can stop us?

- Sing together in your home; no matter how bad you deem your voice to be, if you can sing in the shower, you can sing songs of praise with your children.

- Learn to praise God in your home, together, as a family. The younger the children, the easier this will be, but it is not impossible to learn to praise God even with teens.

- Ask God to release you in the home, to help you to be free and not intimidated by one another or self-conscious. Learn to dance together. If you have flags and banners, use them in your home. If you don't have them, make flags and banners. As an adult, learn to praise God in all situations; learn by practice.

- Use coloured ribbons, drums and percussion instruments. The Bible says to sing and make music to the Lord with dance and with loud instruments (Psalm 150). Psalm 145 says, 'every day I will praise you'. If we save our praise and music making for a church meeting, if we can only do it 'at church', then we are being religious – tied up by a set of rules – and missing the heart of Scripture.

- Learn to model praising and thanking God in any situation. Your children will come home again and again with stories of how someone bullied them, or swore at them or spoke in a nasty way; or stories of how the teacher was unreasonable or unkind. Our responses on those occasions tell our children what we really believe about Jesus beyond what we are trying to teach them. Our responses on those occasions have a far greater impact on our children than what we say we believe. Following is an example.

Example:

Your primary school child comes home and speaks about being bullied. Some would argue we would be within our 'rights' to immediately storm into the school and demand:

an apology,

a punishment for the bully,

that something is done to stop the bullies in this school,

a promise from the head teacher that this will never happen again.

But, what would Jesus do? What does the situation look like through his eyes? What does God's word have to do with this situation? Where is the role of praise and thanksgiving in this situation? Could this be an opportunity to practise a lifestyle of praise, in any and every situation? Following are some suggestions. They are by no means the only way to proceed; however, they have been tried in a real situation and have had positive effects. Some of the following suggestions will be of help in many different situations and not just in the event of bullying.

At some point, we may speak to a classroom teacher or even a head teacher and that will be the right thing to do. It would be sad if that were the only thing we did. Compare the above strong *reaction* to the following response to Jesus:

Tell your child that the real battle is not against the child who is bullying others; it is not us against him or her (Ephesians 6:12).

Tell your child that God loves bullies and pray for the bully together. Ask for God's heart for the bully. You may be surprised at what you feel. Ask for God's touch in the child's life. Pray for his home situation and ask God to move at the level of why the child is a bully. Persevere in this prayer, every week for a school year, if need be.

Come to Jesus with your child and ask his Spirit to fill you both. Ask the Holy Spirit to help your child to be strong and to 'love your enemies' in the situation. Here is a personal testimony. A boy we know was bullied. The parents prayed with him as indicated above on a regular basis. One day the bully began to push the boy's friend around and verbally abuse him. The boy who had prayed marched up to the bully, looked him in the eye and declared in a loud voice, 'You leave my friend alone!' 'Who's going to make me?' countered the bully.

'I'm telling you to go away,' said the little boy. To his utter amazement, the bully backed off and just walked away. This shouldn't have happened; the bully would usually have punched anyone who challenged him. But somehow the presence of God was with the little boy and not only powerfully affected the situation, but changed the little boy's heart so that he was no longer afraid of the bully. The story didn't end there; the boy and his parents continued to pray not only for the bully, but also for opportunities to be kind to him.

- The following suggestions will have a very positive effect in many situations, not just in the event of bullying. What about in the event of sickness, or a major disappointment, or a loss of friendship or even loss of life, or a serious problem in the life of close friends?

Tell your child the truth. God has a way through this situation for your child, where he wants to bring good out of it. We don't only want the bullying to stop, but we want to be salt and light in the situation. We will not stand for our child passively becoming a victim, yet we want to bring some of the kingdom of God into the situation. We want to be ambassadors for Jesus. We want people to know Jesus and to come to salvation. Pray with your child that he or she can be an instrument of God's purposes.

Tell your children that, if they allow him, God will use this difficult situation to build strength, faith and character in their lives. They simply need to yield to him and find his way through the situation. God's way will bring blessing into the situation and will defeat the enemy who wants to bring destruction and trouble and unrest among the children.

Thank God in the situation, because this is an opportunity for your child and not an obstacle. It is an opportunity to grow in faith, one to see Jesus move, one to see the advancing of God's Kingdom and one to see another child touched with the love of God.

Find out what God's word says about this situation. Find Psalms and read them with your child. Use God's word in your difficult situation and watch with amazement the effects.

Find Scriptures about God's greatness, his faithfulness, his strength and his protection. Read those verses with your child and praise God together.

Above all, live in the joy of the Lord; have fun with your children. Let praise be ecstatic, laugh together. Praise God at the most unlikely times. Praise God in radical and unconventional ways.

Example:

A young couple we once knew found themselves in one of London's largest and most beautiful parks one day. Their lives were ordinary, there was nothing special happening and it was a cloudy day. They were not extra religious, but they loved Jesus. Suddenly they found themselves dancing round and round, singing a praise song together, right out in the open.

Asking the couple today what they were singing about, they have no idea; they cannot remember and they feel a bit embarrassed at their antics. But the Lord undoubtedly remembers and was honoured by their simple, some would say even silly, praise. It brings to mind another young man who even offended some of his peers when he danced nearly naked before the Lord, in sheer exuberance (2 Samuel 6).

What do we fill our Minds with?

Practical suggestions for parents: how to help our children respond from a young age to the challenge in Philippians 4:8.

- Philippians 4:8. A challenge to parents: How can I personally respond to this Bible verse? What is God's Spirit saying to me? It is good to be already responding to God's word to us before we begin to challenge our children.

- Challenging one another in the home: There needs to be room in the family setting for mutual challenge, in humility, even in a light-hearted but sincere way. We know that parents often challenge their own children regarding their spiritual diet, but it is also important for parents to be open to being challenged by their children. None of us could boast that we have been totally immune to small areas of hypocrisy in our lives, where what we say is not quite how we live. If our children are the ones to bring these things to our attention, if there is honour and respect in the way we speak with each other in the home, then we can thank God for their insight and our own opportunity to grow.

- Accountability in the home: The Bible speaks of submitting ourselves to one another. Accountability means to simply give an account of ourselves, of our attitudes and our actions. In terms of character development and discipline we function very much in a parent (caregiver, role model, leader, and teacher) child (learner, follower, the nurtured) relationship. However, in terms of being followers of Jesus, we are accountable to our children as they are to us. If we have one standard of behaviour for our children and another standard for ourselves, we will neither deserve nor gain their respect. They may then believe that living by a double standard is the normal way to live. Sin that develops into addiction often does so because it is practised in secrecy. Our lives need to be open to our children. If there are any areas of our lives we would be ashamed our children knew about, perhaps that is an indicator that we may need counsel or repentance and change. How wonderful for our lives to be an open book, where we live simply and with full freedom to both encourage and challenge one another? Following are real illustrations of these two models of accountability, which we have been writing about. Though they refer to church leaders, both attitudes could also apply to parents.

A church leader speaking about being accountable to his flock, because of how he perceived his responsibility before God to live an open and holy life: 'If you see ungodly behaviour in my life, I am open to you challenging me; if what you see is different to what I preach, you have a right to speak to me.' Contrast this with a church leader who believes: 'What I do in my own home is my business and is not open to question or discussion.'

We need to ask ourselves as parents. Is there any way I live that is not open to challenge? Do I live in a different way in the home than I do outside it? Do I read or watch, say anything or listen to anything that I wouldn't want my children or my spouse to know about? Is there any area of my life that is lived in secrecy? Is there pride, where I believe my children don't have a right to question anything I do or say?

- This book is not a platform to express the author's views on what is acceptable viewing, reading or listening. Do we follow after our neighbour's conscience and watch what others watch? The fact is that Jesus is our standard and it should be the Holy Spirit's conviction that motivates us in all we do. The best we can do for our children is to help, model and pray for them to be open to the Holy Spirit's voice in their own lives. Many people in America and the UK have taken to wearing a wristband engraved with the initials WWJD, standing for 'What would Jesus Do?' They simply wear the band to remind them through all the choices and decisions they face on a daily basis.

- We need to remember our freedom in Jesus; we are not encouraging parents to make rigid laws about what is or is not acceptable viewing, reading, playing or listening. Parents may, however, feel that they need certain guidelines or boundaries to operate within their family.

- Discussion in the home: We cannot overemphasise the importance of regular, loving communication and discussion between parents and children regarding these issues. It is not always the best policy to quickly turn off questionable material; that can be like slamming a door in your child's face and they cannot understand why.

A rigid and strong reaction to questionable material, without clear discussion, can provoke an insatiable curiosity in your child and can therefore be damaging. Why not occasionally talk together, watch or listen to some things with your child, explaining why you want to avoid feeding on them. Particularly if it comes up in their lives (i.e. if they see it in the homes of their friends), show them a game that you feel is not edifying. Read small parts of a book together, which they have either come across or brought home from the school library. Show your child why things are not going to be helpful to their spiritual development. Talk with your children – and truly listen to their thoughts and their comments – help them to understand by using illustrations – pray together for God's heart and the Holy Spirit's wisdom.

- Look for and find and use with your children videos, computer games, music, books and television, which are fun, enjoyable, humorous, exciting and challenging. Make sure you present your children with wonderful alternatives and the best of what is available. Ask God for creative inspiration to help feed your children's spirits. Encourage the pursuit of outdoor activities and other hobbies. These options, along with our heartfelt prayers, will definitely cost in time and sometimes money. But this brings us right back to our calling, which is to live by faith and trust God for provision and help in literally every aspect of our lives.

- An interesting perspective on videos, games, computer programs, the Internet and television and their effect on our children is the book, *Children at Risk*, by David Porter (Kingsway, 1986). While I am not necessarily in agreement with all the author's arguments or perspectives, the book is very well researched and not only presents valuable information but exposes many parental stances which are based on fear rather than fact. The book can be a helpful tool in developing a way to walk with our children through the often mesmerising maze of media, marketing and manipulative advertising they face on a daily basis.